AF478020

Atlantic Studies on Society in Change
No. 70

Editor-in-Chief: Béla K. Király
Associate Editor-in-chief: Peter Pastor

Trianon
and the Protection
of Minorities

József Galántai

SOCIAL SCIENCES MONOGRAPHS, BOULDER, COLORADO
ATLANTIC RESEARCH AND PUBLICATIONS,
HIGHLAND LAKES, NEW JERSEY
DISTRIBUTED BY COLUMBIA UNIVERSITY PRESS

1992

East European Monographs No. CCCLII

Library of Congress Catalog Card Number 92-60818
ISBN 0-88033-249-2
Printed in Hungary

Contents

Introduction

When the maps of East Central Europe were redrawn after World War I, Austria-Hungary—that is, each half of the dualist and ethnically diverse Habsburg Monarchy—was divided into component nation-states. The great transformation was supposed to be based on the principle of self-determination, but in fact often violated this principle. Under the new arrangements, thirty percent of the ten-million-strong Hungarian population found themselves living outside Hungary. Nearly one-third of the Hungarians in the Carpathian Basin were thus obliged to lead the life of national minorities in one of the successor states (Romania, Czechoslovakia, Yugoslavia), regardless of the organic links that most of them enjoyed with the central bloc of Hungarians within Hungary itself. *Today these roughly three million Hungarians make up the largest single national minority in East Central Europe.*

The process of national reorganization in East Central Europe was sanctioned by the Paris Peace Conference, which convened after World War I, in the treaties of Versailles (with Germany), Saint-Germain (with Austria), Trianon (with Hungary), Neuilly (with Bulgaria), and Sèvres—later Lausanne—(with Turkey). In addition to altering the frontiers of existing states and drawing the borders of new ones, the treaties also made provision for the protection of national minorities in the countries involved. The principal powers at the Peace Conference (the British Empire, France, the United States, Italy, and Japan) all signed international conventions with the states benefiting from the territorial changes (Poland, Czechoslovakia, Romania, Yugoslavia, Greece) concerning the rights of national minorities. These conventions were guaranteed by the League of Nations (the predecessor of the United Nations established by the Peace Conference), and were reinforced by similar passages incorporated in the peace treaties themselves.

Thus, the minority rights guaranteed under international law were regarded by the Principal Powers at the Peace Conference as an organic and indispensable element in the new state system of East Central Europe. To overcome the reluctance of the new majority nations, Woodrow Wilson, president of the United States, emphasized the need to link the two issues at the plenary meeting of the Peace Conference held on May 31, 1919:

> We are trying to make a peaceful settlement, that is to say, to eliminate those elements of disturbance, so far as possible, which may interfere with the peace of the world... Take the rights of the minorities. Nothing, I venture to say, is more likely to disturb the peace of the world than the treatment which might in certain circumstances be meted out to minorities. And, therefore, if the great powers are to guarantee the peace of the world in any sense is it unjust that they should be satisfied that the proper and necessary guarantee has been given?

The internationally-guaranteed system of minority rights in East Central Europe worked effectively during the following fifteen years. It was swept away by the rise of fascism in Europe, and, unfortunately, was not reinstated by the peace conference which concluded World War II.

In the present book the author wishes to shed some light on this long-forgotten aspect of the remaking of East Central Europe, an aspect which at one time constituted an organic part of it. History does not repeat itself, and even the old questions are continually in need of new answers; but the study of history can, perhaps, provide useful lessons for the addressing of current problems.

Chapter 1
The Restructuring of the State System of East Central Europe and of National Minority Relations after World War I

The Specific Character of "East Central Europe"

The region specified by the term "East Central Europe" is bordered on one side by large German and Italian populations and on the other by Russians, Ukrainians, and Byelorussians. Within this zone, which lies between vast eastern and western regions and which stretches from the Barents Sea to the Mediterranean, a mixture of small ethnic groups and a diversity of religious denominations have for many centuries been characteristic features. In the period covered by this book a large bloc of Orthodox-Slavic peoples (Russians, Ukrainians, and Byelorussians) in the East and extensive Italian and German populations in the West were separated by a strip of territory inhabited by a lot of smaller nations and ethnic groups, of which even the larger were of diminutive size in comparison to their great neighbors. This has been one of the most important characteristics of the East Central European region, and has had a bearing on its entire history. In fact, the expression "East Central Europe" is used as a historical rather than as a geographical definition, and it was precisely this ethnic and religious pluralism that gave meaning to the concept.

In the first decade of the twentieth century, when the population of Europe totaled 450 to 500 millions, this ethnically varied zone contained 100 to 120 million inhabitants.

It is worth examining the ethnic composition of the region's population. However, it should be mentioned that there exist no precise statistical surveys to help in this. No single definition of "nationality" was employed in the surveys: the criteria applied in deciding the nationality of individuals changed from one survey to the next. Some of the statistical surveys defined nationality on the basis of language, and these seem to be the most reliable. Even so, such a method was not without its problems; for example, in the case of bilingual people, the various surveys used differing methods to establish the first language. Of the surveys covering the entire region, it is best to rely on Dr. Wilhelm Winkler's *Statistisches Handbuch der europäischen Nationalitäten,* published in 1931, and on C. A. Macartney's *National States and National Minorities,* published in 1934. These works give the population levels of the various nationalities of East Central Europe in the first decades of the twentieth century as follows (entries are in alphabetical order, and figures are rounded off):

Albanians	1.4 million	Lithuanians	1.8 million
Austrians[+]	6.8 million	Hungarians	10 million
Bulgarians	5 million	Poles	20 million
Croats	2.7 million	Romanians	12 million
Czechs	7 million	Serbs	6.2 million
Estonians	1 million	Slovaks	2.2 million
Finns	2.8 million	Slovenes	1.4 million
Greeks	6 million	Turks[++]	1.8 million
Latvians	1.4 million		

[+] In addition to the 6.5 million German-speaking population of Austria, only the German minority living in Italy (280,000) is included in this category. German minorities living elsewhere, including those in Bohemia, Moravia, and Austrian Silesia (all formerly part of Austria), regarded Germany, rather than Austria, as their "mother-nation."

[++] Of course, only the Turkish population in Europe, including Istanbul, is included here.

Any statistical survey showing the region's national and ethnic composition would not be complete without mention of the millions of Germans dispersed throughout the zone (nearly eight million people in the 1920s), and of the millions of Jews who spoke Yiddish (more than six million people).*

The internal heterogeneity typical of the region, and evident from a glance at the above table, was further complicated by the intense mixing of the small nations or ethnic groups and the larger peoples of the neighboring countries. When those affected by the latter process are taken into account, some additional millions (from among the Ukrainians, Russians, Byelorussians, Swedes,

---

* The number of Jews in the region was—if calculated not on the basis of mother-tongue, but on that of religion—considerably higher (nearly three million higher), since this wider category also included assimilated Jews.

and Italians) can be added to the population constituted by the mixed ethnic and national groups living in the region.

The internal heterogeneity of the area is, of course, obvious, but it only becomes striking when seen in the context of the neighboring regions of Europe. Only slightly more people (120 million) lived in the part of Europe lying east of this belt (i.e. east as far as the Ural and the Caucasian mountains) than lived in the East Central European belt itself. Yet, 65 million of these were Russians, 30 million were Ukrainians, and 4.5 million were Byelorussians; in other words, 60 per cent of the population belonged to one nationality, and 86 per cent to one of the three largest peoples, which were closely related through their languages and history. When we make the same comparison with the region on the other side of the belt, the ethnic diversity of "Intermediate Europe" will, again, become clear. The western neighbors included the 65 million-strong German nation, the Italians numbering 35 million, and the Swedes who numbered six million.* This population was only slightly larger than that of East Central Europe, yet when it came to ethnic diversity, it was not in the same league.

When we consider the entire European region west of the East Central European belt (240 million inhabitants), we find that the four largest nations (Germany, Britain, France, and Italy) accounted for 70 percent of the entire population of the region.

Therefore, it was the national composition of its eastern and western neighbors that underlined the most salient feature of East Central Europe at this time, namely its national and ethnic confusion.

---

* At first glance, the six-million-strong Swedish population does not seem to be particularly large in comparison with some nationalities in the East Central European belt. However, when this population is compared with the population of its immediate neighbors (Finland and the Baltic States), the above-mentioned contrast once again becomes striking. The contrast is also apparent in economic development, which would set Sweden, a country with a thriving economy comparable to the most advanced Western states, further apart from even the largest nations of East Central Europe.

The Historical Background

Rather than being created by some sudden historical change, the present national and ethnic complexity of "Intermediate Europe" came about through a centuries-long historical process (which in itself was another basic characteristic of the region), although it acquired a clear significance only in recent times. Ethnic and linguistic divisions and the relative balance of the various groups were much less important under the feudal system than they later became in the age of national development and organization.

The governing Polish, Lithuanian, Czech, Hungarian, and Bulgarian nobilities were not only able to establish and maintain feudal states—as did other more numerous groups—, but could, at least for a while, conquer considerable additional territories as well. In the Modern Age, however, the kingdoms and empires of the area required more solid popular and national foundations —supported by the necessary economies—than the smaller states in the area could command. In more recent times, none of the aforementioned nations was able to establish such constructs, and one after another all succumbed to empires supported by hinterlands outside the area.

By the beginning of the nineteenth century, there was not one independent state remaining in East Central Europe; the entire region was dominated by the four empires established by outsider nations. It is worth considering briefly the process which brought about this state of affairs. The demise of the system of independent kingdoms took place over a period of two to three hundred years. First the Asian-based Ottoman Empire delivered a series of blows to those kingdoms which were either totally independent or in loose feudal vassalage in the southern parts of the East Central European belt. By the mid-sixteenth century the Ottoman Turks had conquered the whole of the Balkans and, after bringing down the independent Kingdom of Hungary, extended their rule to Buda and then almost to Vienna.

Subsequent expansion of the Ottoman Empire was checked by the Habsburg Monarchy. Capable of drawing on the strength of the Holy Roman Empire, the Habsburg Monarchy rose rapidly, first acquiring the lands of the Hungarian Crown and then those of the Czech kingdom. This newly-emerging power in East Central Europe, besides affording some protection against the Turks, served to control the subject-nations it acquired.

From the sixteenth century, dominion over the southern and central regions of East Central Europe was shared between two empires. The Balkan peoples were struggling under the Ottoman yoke; and the lands of the Hungarian and the Czech crowns passed to the Habsburgs, who halted Ottoman expansionism in East Central Europe through their ability to concentrate considerable forces, but who regarded the newly-acquired territories as conquered land.

During the same centuries the imperial ambitions of the great neighbor to the east were also growing rapidly. In the eighteenth-century tsarist Russia wrested the Baltic States and Finland from Swedish suzerainty, and then extended its control to Lithuania.

The last state in the East Central European belt to lose independence was Poland. In the second half of the eighteenth century its territory was gradually divided between Russia, the Habsburg Monarchy, and the increasingly powerful Kingdom of Prussia. By the beginning of the nineteenth century the division of the East Central European belt between the four outside states was complete.

The nineteenth century was, however, already characterized by bourgeois and national development, which strengthened the desire in the various nationalities for freedom and self-determination. The four powers which ruled East Central Europe found themselves challenged; they reacted first by giving a demonstration of strength, then by granting minor concessions in face of the new demands.

The Ottoman Empire, based in Asia and a captive of its own feudal structure, was least able to adjust to the changes. It adamantly rejected national aspirations in the Balkans, although it no longer had power to suppress them with any lasting effect. Within the Ottoman Empire, the first successful war of independence was fought by the Greeks, and this led, with the support of the West European powers, to the establishment of an independent national state. Soon after, similar attempts by the Serbs and the Romanians were crowned with success: although still formally linked to the Porte, both nations set up their own states by cleverly exploiting the Balkan rivalries of the Great Powers. But the greater part of the peninsula—Bulgaria, Bosnia, Herzegovina, Macedonia, and Thrace—still remained under direct Turkish rule, and the next wave of liberation came only with the 1848 revolutions. In these the Habsburg Monarchy was severely shaken. True, Habsburg control could be re-established for a short period, but in the long run Italian unification could not be averted: Lombardy and Venetia were united with Piedmont, and Hungary's subordinate position within the Monarchy ended with the introduction, in 1867, of a dualist system founded on a partnership between the two strongest nations. The mid-nine-teenth-century revolutions in Central Europe solved the German, Italian, and Hungarian problems, or at least pointed towards a solution, but they did not provide answers to most of the questions concerning the other nations in East Central Europe.

When one looks at the map of East Central Europe just before World War I, and compares it with the situation prevailing a century earlier, one finds that despite some substantial changes, the dependency of the region was more or less the same. By this time a number of small independent states had appeared in the Balkans: Greece, Serbia, Romania, and, after the 1870s and 1880s, Bulgaria. During the First Balkan War (in 1912) the joint forces of these states pushed the Turks almost entirely out of the peninsula. And although this undoubtedly represented a big step forward, the Balkans more than ever became the focus for interference by the Great Powers. The fact that Habsburg absolutism became tempered with liberalism and that the Monarchy evolved into a dualist state can also be seen as representing a step forward; nevertheless, the majority of the peoples living in it remained dependent. The emancipation of the serfs in Russia (in 1861) also indicated a slight advance for liberalism, but the division of Poland and the dependence of Finland and the Baltic States continued. Thus, in the early years of the twentieth century, when Austria-Hungary, Germany and Russia ruled the greater part of East Central Europe, this challenge, reinforced by bourgeois and national evolution, posed an increasingly serious threat to these three states.

The Catalyst of Change: World War I

As a result of World War I, its aftermath, and some more deeply-rooted factors, the political geography of the East Central European region underwent complete transformation.

In late July and early August 1914, when the leading politicians of the great continental powers were considering the chances of a war, the prevailing view in government circles was that a brief campaign of the traditional kind was to be anticipated. Each general staff believed that by fully exploiting the possibilities of speedier mobilization, rapid deployment, and more effective artillery power, the fighting could soon be brought to an end. The German general staff was convinced that, having overrun Belgium, the numerically superior right flank of the German forces would destroy the entire French army in two months at the most. The French generals believed that, pushing through Alsace-Lorraine with all available forces, they could march straight to Berlin, concluding the entire war within a couple of months. The Russian general staff anticipated a slightly longer campaign running to a maximum of four months. Because mobilization would be less swift, some time would be needed before the mighty Russian "steamroller" could begin its advance westward, but once it was set in motion the final victory, they believed, would not be long in coming. Austria-Hungary's general staff calculated that the German forces would beat the French in six weeks, and then, having linked up with the Austro-Hungarian armies on the eastern front, would end the war by scoring a final and decisive victory there. Serbia would subsequently be crushed.

All the parties concerned thought that after a quick victory it would be up to the politicians to establish a new balance of power in Europe, a balance of power based on the new military situation. The German political leadership planned a comprehensive redrawing of the map of Europe and the creation of a *Mitteleuropa* under German hegemony. The Entente powers wished to defeat German imperialism and its bid for 'world domination,' but without introducing substantial changes in the European status quo. There was nothing in the original plans of the Entente Powers to suggest that far-reaching changes were contemplated in the state system of East Central Europe. Naturally, frontiers might need to be altered as a result of victory on the battlefield, but the system of states would, for the most part, be preserved.

The various general staffs, however, misjudged the effectiveness of the new weapons. The military commanders thought that the greater fire-power and improved mobility of the troops would only assist their offensive capabilities, leading them to believe that the war would end quickly. In fact precisely the opposite was demonstrated in the bloody battles which followed the start of hostilities. The quick-firing field gun, the machine-gun and a more efficient rifle all improved the quality of the defense. Well dug in and adequately armed, defending troops proved virtually insuperable, and could hold out against superior numbers for a considerable length of time. Although the technical superiority of the Entente became clear after the initial German and Austro-Hungarian offensives, the war dragged on. Victory on the battlefield could only be achieved through attrition—that is, if the numerical superiority of the attacking forces was such that they could overwhelm the defense, despite the latter's positional advantages. The blockaded Central Powers, however, had enormous resources—resources which they consumed to the full. This process took a good many years.

Consequently, the war ceased to be a battle between the opposing soldiers and their weaponry; rather it became a battle between the resources in the respective hinterlands. It pushed the production capabilities of the warring nations to their limit, especially in the Central Powers and in Russia—states whose resources were more modest. After more than four years of fighting only the replacement of Russia by the United States could produce a final military victory for the Entente.

By autumn 1918 the guns had fallen silent and the winners and losers had emerged. But the world, and especially Europe, had undergone considerable changes during the hostilities—changes in more ways than one. The hierarchy of the most powerful nations altered. Great Britain, formerly the world's leading power, lost prestige. Germany and Russia were—temporarily at least—forced out of the running: the former by its defeat, the latter by its confusion. The prestige of the United States as a world power increased. There was another big change: Russia, a great power which had been undergoing dynamic development since

1900, was now a center of social revolution. A similarly-important new development was the disturbance of the colonial world, which had been dragged into the European conflict. This showed itself in the beginnings of upheaval in China and India. Last, but by no means least, in the midst of these historical changes and in interaction with them, the status quo was thoroughly changed in East Central Europe, one of the focal points of the emerging new world order.

Initially, British, French, and Russian policy had made no allowances for fundamental changes in the region. Originally, neither the liberation of Finland and the Baltic States from Russia, nor the restoration of Poland's independence, nor the abolition of the Habsburg Monarchy was intended; nevertheless, after the war all these changes actually took place and received endorsement. The Entente powers had begun a more serious formulation and harmonization of their European war aims just four months into the fighting, still believing that after the successful repulse of enemy offensives and the complete deployment of friendly forces, final victory would soon be theirs. From the synchronization of plans it appears that at this time fundamental changes in the status quo of East Central Europe were not intended. The region would continue to be divided between Russia, Germany, and the Habsburg Monarchy, although some Polish territory annexed to Germany and Austria-Hungary, as well as the Ukrainian territory then governed by Vienna, would have gone to Russia, while, in the south, Serbia would acquire Bosnia-Herzegovina. In addition, there were plans for the internal reorganization of the Habsburg Monarchy, although these would not have altered the basic dimensions of imperial rule in the region. This is hardly surprising, given that one precondition for the rearrangement of the region was the fall of tsarist Russia and an end to its expansionism. In 1914, when the war started, Russia was itself an Entente power; accordingly, a rapid Entente victory could not have led to the curtailment of its regional interests. If anything, the opposite would be expected. Great Britain and France, in order to counter the growth of Russian influence in the region, thought it necessary that, after its detachment from Germany, the Habsburg Monarchy should be allowed to preserve its power.

Therefore, when one investigates the factors leading to the

complete rearrangement of the East Central European belt, one does not find them among the original war aims of the Entente Powers. A better indication is provided by the national aspirations already present in the region, the most important of which was the desire of the various nationalities to cast off their subordinate position within the empires and to achieve statehood of their own. In each case this concept of statehood was based on "historic" rights or on a claim for national supremacy within a larger state, rather than on narrower ethnic or linguistic principles. In these national movements the idea of a thorough reorganization of the region always featured in some form or another. In the first year of the war, such national thinking could chiefly be detected in the aspirations of Czech and Croat émigré circles, as well as in Polish ambitions. The program linking the war to a fundamental reorganization of the region was, therefore, manifest in the policies of the émigré circles even at the beginning of the war, although at that time it did not predominate in the home-based national movements of the region. Without yet supporting the long-term aims of the émigré circles, the Entente states from the very beginning utilized their influence to subvert the enemy and to encourage desertions.

With the war dragging on, the Entente powers were more and more obliged to take the national movements into account in order to find new allies. The need to win over Italy, Romania, and Greece steered the Entente towards promises and treaties that pointed increasingly to a re-alignment of East Central Europe. Furthermore, the fact that the two multinational empires, Russia and Austria-Hungary, were the least able to bear the internal tensions exacerbated by the war contributed towards the same outcome. Their deepening domestic crises strengthened these national movements, which were striving for a radical re-ordering of the state system. To the principal Entente powers the goodwill of these movements became indispensable not only to the successful ending of hostilities, but also to postwar consolidation.

The Restructuring of East Central Europe

The collapse of the old system of states in East Central Europe during the final phase of World War I and the months following the armistice was dramatic indeed; the foundations of the system replacing it took shape concurrently. The principal states of the new system were the small powers allied to the Entente: Poland, Romania, Czechoslovakia, and Yugoslavia. On one hand these states seemed the most interested in the construction of a new system aimed at bringing stability to the region; on the other hand, they were also the countries which most readily fitted in with the Entente's foreign policy plans for the new Europe. In addition they were intended to constitute a barrier against any Russian or German expansionism. Nevertheless, these key states would have been far too small and weak had they been built exclusively on ethnicity. Thus, national aspirations which extended the respective state-concepts far beyond the ethnic principle coincided with the ambitions of the leading Entente powers, which wished to stabilize the region in line with their own interests. The new national states, instead of being limited to a narrow nationality base, needed to be relatively strong and large formations—in the creation of which economic and strategic considerations were similarly important. Acceptance of such thinking meant that these states would inevitably incorporate sizeable national minorities. Accordingly, the new order in East Central Europe —based as it was on four states, each one with sizeable national minorities—was not so very different from that which prevailed before. At the birth of the old system the four dominant empires had been able to draw on their external hinterlands; in the new system the four key multinational states enjoyed not only external, but also internal support.

History played an interesting role in all this. Initially, as we have seen, the British Empire, France, and the United States (which joined the war in April 1917) had no intention of changing the system of states in East Central Europe. The frequent mention of the duty to protect the small nationalities was perhaps serious only in the case of Belgium and Serbia; otherwise, it amounted to mere ideological sloganizing aimed more at the internal liberalization and the federalization of the multinational empires. Although the Entente's plans said nothing about the restructuring of the region, the actual moves made in the interests of victory —the support given to the émigré circles, the secret treaties securing new allies (the Treaty of London with Italy in 1915; the Treaty of Bucharest with Romania in 1916), as well as ideology (the right to self-determination)—all encouraged the nationality movements. The process of rearrangement that followed the war was, although not directly orchestrated by the Great Powers, nevertheless, in no way contrary to their wishes. The Peace Settlement merely sanctioned the changes: the war destroyed the essence of the old system. As David Hunter Miller, a prominent member of the United States peace delegation, remarked, the important decisions had all been made and "no Peace Conference, nothing but armed Force, could have reunited" the old states.[1]

Writing more than fifteen years later, David Lloyd George also referred to the importance of the autonomous action on the part of Austria-Hungary's subject-nations, pointing out that the Entente powers, rather than themselves initiating the changes, simply followed events:

The tearing up of the Austrian Empire into disparate and unconnected fragments was no part of the policy of France, Russia, Britain, America, or Italy. We knew there must be readjustment of frontiers in favour of Italy, Serbia, and Roumania. As for the rest of the Austrian Empire, the idea that found favour was...: the conferring of complete autonomy on the component races who made up the Austro-Hungarian Empire, inside a federal constitution... Ere the Powers came to consider the Austrian Peace they were confronted with accomplished and irreversible facts... The task of the Parisian treaty makers was not to decide what in fairness should be given to the liberated nationalities, but what in common honesty should be freed from their clutches when they had overstepped the bounds of self-determination.[2]

The National Minorities in the New System of States

At the Peace Conference the newly-established states of East Central Europe received sanction, and their precise borders were drawn. These states, however, had been formed at the end of the war, and were already effectively in operation by the time the Peace Conference convened. It therefore makes sense that before discussing the work of the Peace Conference, we review the structure of the new system of states in East Central Europe from the standpoint of the minority issue.

This re-alignment in the region is usually referred to in the historiography as the "formation of a system of national states." In reality, the majority of these new state formations were, like the empires preceding them, multinational in character. Before 1914 half of the inhabitants of East Central Europe, some fifty million people, lived the life of minorities or subject-peoples. After the realignment, this number fell to 32 million, nearly one-third of the entire population of the region. In this sense the national concept, as a force for change, was indeed at work: sovereignty was conferred on a number of peoples which previously had subordinate status, while other former subject-peoples became the majority in their new states. Still, in a number of cases the re-alignment failed to produce national states, as some of the new constructs represented the joining together of several different peoples; and the national minorities as a percentage of total population remained high in each new or enlarged country.

The above statements can be illustrated with the help of two tables. The first shows the ethnic composition of the countries, and the relative sizes of the majority and the minority peoples. The second table lists all the nationalities living in the region, giving both their total population and a population breakdown of each country concerned.

It has already been mentioned that these statistics conceal a great many ambiguities. Nevertheless, the following Tables, despite their inaccuracies, are well-suited to showing the distribution of national minorities in the newly-formed or newly-augmented states.

Table 1
THE STATES OF POSTWAR EAST CENTRAL EUROPE
AND THE NATIONAL-LINGUISTIC MINORITIES INHABITING
THE INDIVIDUAL STATES*

Country (year)**	Total population	Majority people	Minority people	Minority breakdown
Finland (1920)	3,100,000	2,750,000 88.7 %	350,000 11.3 %	343,000 Swedes 5,000 Russians 2,000 Germans
Estonia (1922)	1,100,000	970,000 88 %	130,000 12 %	91,000 Russians 18,000 Germans 8,000 Swedes 8,000 Lithuanians 5,000 Jews***
Latvia (1930)	1,900,000	1,400,000 74 %	500,000 26 %	203,000 Russians 95,000 Jews 70,000 Germans 62,000 Poles 36,000 Byelorussians 26,000 Lithuanians 8,000 Estonians
Lithuania (including the Memelland) (1925)	2,170,000	1,740,000 80.2 %	430,000 19.8 %	154,000 Jews 140,000 Germans (including *Memellers*) 66,000 Poles 51,000 Russians 15,000 Latvians 4,000 Byelorussians
Danzig (1923)	365,000	350,000 95.9 %	15,000 4.1 %	15,000 Poles

* In addition to the earlier-mentioned volumes by Winkler and Macartney, extensive use has been made of the statistical information published in Oscar Janowsky's *Nationalities and National Minorities with Special Reference to East Central Europe* (New York, 1945) and in volume 2 of *Atlas zur Weltgeschichte*. 20th ed. (München, 1985).

** The year shown in brackets refers to the time the census was taken.

*** As before, the term "Jews" refers to people speaking Yiddish rather than those professing Judaism. Of course, lack of reliable surveys and the difficulties inherent in making such surveys mean that the figures given should be regarded as estimates.

Country	Total	Majority	Minority	Minority
Poland (1931)	32,000,000	22,000,000 68.8 %	10,000,000 31.2 %	4,070,000 Ukrainians 3,000,000 Jews 1,500,000 Byelorussians 1,100,000 Germans 200,000 Russians 100,000 Lithuanians 30,000 Czechs
Czecho-slovakia (1930)	14,085,000	7,200,000 Czechs + 2,000,000 Slovaks = 9,200,000 65.4 %	4,885,000 34.6 %	3,300,000 Germans 700,000 Hungarians 590,000 Ukrainians 190,000 Jews 90,000 Poles 15,000 Romanians
Austria	6,490,000	6,275,000 96.7 %	215,000 3.3 %	95,000 Czechs 45,000 Croats and Serbs 45,000 Slovenes 25,000 Hungarians 5,000 Slovaks
Hungary	7,980,000	7,150,000 89.6 %	830,000 10.4 %	590,000 Germans 142,000 Slovaks 37,000 Croats 37,000 Serbs and other South Slavs 24,000 Romanians
Romania (1930)	18,000,000	12,815,000 71.2 %	5,185,000 28.8 %	1,900,000 Hungarians 950,000 Jews 720,000 Germans 550,000 Ukrainians 400,000 Bulgarians 200,000 Turks and Tartars 150,000 Russians 135,000 Gypsieslll l60,000 Serbs 50,000 Poles 50,000 Slovaks (and Czechs) 10,000 Greeks 10,000 Armenians
Kingdom of Serbs, Croats and Slovenes	12,012,000	5,000,000 Serbs + 3,500,000	2,487,000	600,000 Macedonians (including Bulgarians) 520,000 Germans

Country	Total	Majority	Minority	Minority
(after 1929: Yugoslavia) (1921)	Croats +	1,025,000 Slovenes = 9,525,000 79.3 %	20.7 %	480,000 Hungarians 450,000 Albanians 235,000 Romanians 120,000 Czechs and Slovaks 60,000 other Slavs 12,000 Spanish-speaking Jews 10,000 Italians
Albania	900,000	820,000 91.2%	80.000 8.8%	60.000 Greeks 20,000 Slavs and others
Bulgaria (1926)	5,450,000	4,575,000 84 %	875,000 16 %	580,000 Turks 140,000 Gypsies 70,000 Romanians 45,000 Jews 20,000 Russians 10,000 Greeks 6,000 Armenians 4,000 Germans
Greece (1928)	6,200,000	5,765,000 93 %	435,000 7 %	190,000 Turks 95,000 Bulgarians and Macedonians 65,000 Spanish-speaking Jews 35,000 Armenians 20,000 Albanians 19,000 Kutzo-Wallachians 5,000 Gypsies 3,000 Russians 3,000 Italians
Turkey (European Turkey only)	1,040,000	830,000 79.8 %	210,000 20.2 %	85,000 Greeks 45,000 Jews (Spanish-speaking or Yiddish-speaking) 38,000 Armenians 12,000 Bulgarians 11,000 French, Italians and Britons 7,000 Albanians 6,000 Arabs, Kurds, Persians and Tartars 6,000 others
	112,792,000	86,165,000 76.4 %	26,627,000 23.6 %	

Table 2
**THE NATIONAL MINORITIES IN POSTWAR EAST CENTRAL
EUROPE AND THEIR DISTRIBUTION AMONG STATES**
(in descending order of population size)*

Minority	Total population	Distribution	
Germans	7,674,000	Czechoslovakia	3,300,000
		Poland	1,100,000
		Soviet Union (the western parts)	930,000
		Romania	720,000
		Hungary	590,000
		Yugoslavia	520,000
		Italy (the northern parts)	280,000
		Lithuania	140,000
		Latvia	70,000
		Estonia	18,000
		Bulgaria	4,000
		Finland	2,000
Jews**	6,411,000	Poland	3,000,000
		Soviet Union (the western parts, mainly the Ukraine)	1,850,000
		Romania	950,000
		Czechoslovakia (mainly Sub-Carpathian Ruthenia)	190,000
		Lithuania	154,000
		Latvia	95,000
		Greece	65,000
		Bulgaria	45,000
		Turkey	145,000
		Yugoslavia	12,000
		Estonia	5,000
Ukrainians	5,210,000	Poland	4,070,000
		Czechoslovakia	5590,000
		Romania	550,000

---

* Unlike the previous one, this table also lists the national minorities living along the western edges of Russia and in the eastern parts of Sweden, Germany, and Italy that are related to the peoples inhabiting the East Central European belt. Nationalities with a population numbering fewer than 50,000 are not listed (Finns, Latvians, Italians, Kutzo-Wallachians, etc.)

** See footnote on page 2.

Minority	Total population	Distribution	
Hungarians	3,112,000	Romania	1,900,000
		Czechoslovakia	700,000
		Yugoslavia	480,000
		Austria	25,000
		Italy	7,000
Byelorussians	1,540,000	Poland	1,500,000
		Latvia	36,000
		Lithuania	4,000
Bulgarians and Macedonians	1,107,000	Yugoslavia	600,000
		Romania	400,000
		Greece	95,000
		Turkey	12,000
Poles	1,513,000	Germany	900,000
		Russia	330,000
		Czechoslovakia	90,000
		Lithuania	66,000
		Latvia	62,000
		Romania	50,000
		Free City of Danzig	15,000
Turks	970,000	Bulgaria	580,000
		Romania	200,000
		Greece	190,000
Russians	755,000	Latvia	203,000
		Poland	200,000
		Romania	150,000
		Estonia	91,000
		Lithuania	51,000
		Germany	32,000
		Bulgaria	20,000
		Finland	5,000
		Greece	3,000
Romanians	594,000	Russia	250,000
		Yugoslavia	235,000
		Bulgaria	70,000
		Hungary	24,000
		Czechoslovakia	15,000
Albanians	571,000	Yugoslavia	450,000
		Italy	94,000
		Greece	20,000
		Turkey	7,000
Czechs and Slovaks	489,000	Hungary	142,000
		Yugoslavia	120,000
		Austria	100,000
		Romania	50,000

Minority	Total population	Distribution	
Serbs and Croats	459,000	Germany	47,000
		Poland	30,000
		Italy	280,000
		Hungary	74,000
		Romania	60,000
		Austria	45,000
Slovenes	395,000	Italy	350,000
		Austria	45,000
Swedes	351,000	Finland	343,000
		Estonia	8,000
Gypsies	280,000*	Bulgaria	140,000
		Romania	135,000
		Greece	5,000
Greeks	165,000	Turkey	85,000
		Albania	60,000
		Bulgaria	10,000
		Romania	10,000
Lithuanians	133,000	Poland	100,000
		Latvia	26,000
		Germany	7,000
Estonians	108,000	Soviet Union	100,000
		Latvia	8,000
Armenians	89,000	Turkey	38,000
		Greece	35,000
		Romania	10,000
		Bulgaria	6,000
Total:	31,926,000		

The two tables yield substantially different totals for the number of people living a minority existence; the difference between them is five million. This can be explained as follows. In the first table only those people were considered who belonged to a minority *in one of the states of the region*. But, in addition, the same minorities had members living a minority life *in one of the great states close by the region*—members who are included in the second table. The total population living a minority existence in "Intermediate Europe" in the years following World War I is more accurately expressed by the second figure. Accordingly,

---

* Undoubtedly, the numbers were considerably higher; however, in most of the countries under review, Gypsies were left out of statistical surveys.

under the new territorial arrangements, one person in three in the region belonged to a minority grouping. This figure accurately reflected the specific situation of the Hungarians: altogether 10,262,000 Hungarians lived in East Central Europe, of whom 7,150,000 (69.7 percent) lived in Hungary and 3,112,000 (30.3 percent) formed minorities in other states. Although this ratio was almost the same as the average for the region as a whole, in the case of most other nationality groups a considerably smaller percentage lived as minorities. Only the Albanians, the Slovenes and the Byelorussians had a situation similar to that of the Hungarians. Accordingly, the Hungarian people found itself at the very center of the minority problem.

Chapter 2
The Importance of the Minorities Problem
in the Plans for Restructuring

The "Key States" and the Minorities

In the last year of the war, the principal Entente powers were already expecting a comprehensive re-alignment of states in East Central Europe, with the implication that a few states in the new power structure would include sizeable national minorities. It was then that the need to protect these minorities came into focus; and the conviction grew that such protection would have to be based on, and guaranteed by, international law if it was to be effective.

The four largest states in the new power system were Poland, Romania, Czechoslovakia, and Yugoslavia.* These were also the states with the largest national minority populations. In Czechoslovakia the minorities amounted to 34.6 percent of the population (the Czechs and Slovaks together constituted the majority people), in Poland 31.2 percent, in Romania 28.8 percent, and in Yugoslavia 20.7 percent (the Serbs, Croats, and Slovenes were regarded as forming the majority grouping). Translating these percentages into totals, we arrive at a minority population of these countries amounting to 10 million, 5.1 million, 4.9 and 2.5 million people respectively. When all the states of the region are taken into account, these minority population figures were the highest.

Of the 113 million inhabitants of the fifteen states in the region (if, for the time being, we ignore those who lived in the mixed population zones across the borders of the great neighboring states to the west and east, but if we include the population of Danzig and those living in the European part of Turkey) 76 million people (67 percent of the total population) lived in these four states. Furthermore, these four states served as a home for

---

* Although, territorially speaking, Finland also qualified as a large state in comparison to the other states of the region, much of its land was uninhabitable and its total population was low.

85 percent of the 26.6 million people who belonged to national minorities in the same fifteen states—some 22.5 million individuals.

This data should also make it clear that in this region any state claiming to be national in the true sense of the word needed to be relatively small. The formation of states of comparatively large area and population was, on the other hand, possible on some kind of federal basis, with the incorporation of large minorities. Yet, in order to fulfill the role expected of them in the new power system, main states had to be strong, and to enjoy a basis broader than that provided by their own majority ethnic populations. From the above it should be obvious that the internal structures in these four states largely—although not exclusively—determined the minority problem in the region.

We saw in the previous chapter that the destruction of the earlier East Central European system of states and its replacement with a new one was originally not a military objective of the principal Entente powers. Nevertheless, the old system of states could only have survived had the three empires dominating the region emerged from the war in a sufficiently strong condition. The drawn-out nature of the conflict and the fact that it continued to the bitter end meant, however, that these empires exhausted all their reserves.

The removal of German influence from East Central Europe was an original Entente military objective; the dismemberment of the other two powers in the region, the Habsburg Monarchy and tsarist Russia, was not. Yet, as Germany's defeat and its banishment from the area was also accompanied by the shattering of the strength of these two states (and in fact ending their presence in East Central Europe), any decision concerning the states which were to constitute the basis of the new power system in East Central Europe had to be in terms of Poland, Czechoslovakia, Romania, and Yugoslavia, since their peoples had helped determine the outcome of the war on the side of the Entente. In theory, a possible alternative could have been an arrangement based on a democratic federation of the nations living in the region, although this would have depended on the spread of successful and enduring democratic revolutions there. Such revolutions did not take place, and their promotion was not incorporated into the policies of the Entente. This alternative was only supported by marginal elements within the socialist and democratic movements. (Oszkár Jászi's vision of a Danubian confederation fell into this category.[1] Jászi's plan, however, was utterly lacking in support: the national revolutions and the Entente were set on a different course.)

Although the Entente powers did not initiate the re-alignment, they were not willing to stand idly by while the process unfolded. They were confronted by the inevitability of radical changes and, indeed, of a new system of states, although the Great Powers still enjoyed considerable opportunities for influence.

We have seen how the national movements and forces helping the establishment of the key states in East Central Europe tended to lay claim to territories far in excess of those which were justifiable on the principle of self-determination. This tendency followed from the nature of the national movements, but interference by the Great Powers could either reinforce or moderate it.

In addition to uniting Poles in an independent state, the Polish national movement also wished to extend Poland's frontiers westward and northward, to include regions populated by Germans, and to the east and the southeast, into territories inhabited by Russians, Lithuanians, Byelorussians, and Ukrainians.

Romanian demands were similarly ambitious, and far exceeded the establishment of a sovereign state uniting the principal Romanian-inhabited areas. The Romanians advocated expansion westward towards Hungarian and Serbian populations, as well as northwards and eastward into Ukrainian territories.

Czech demands, too, were not modest. Prague wanted more than the mere union of the Czech and Slovak peoples in a sovereign state: Prague cast covetous eyes on regions populated by millions of Germans and by hundreds of thousands of Hungarians.

Nor were the ambitions of the South Slav federation any different in this respect; they pointed far beyond the joining of the Serb, Croat, and Slovene peoples. Not satisfied with the annexation of Albanian and the Macedonian regions in the Balkan Wars of 1912–13, the new state demanded additional areas settled by Bulgarian, Hungarian, and Austro-German populations.

The American diplomat H. Gibson, fresh from a tour with an

American delegation through the lands of the former Monarchy, sent a remarkable report, dated February 1, 1919, to U.S. Secretary of State Robert L. Lansing, then in Paris. In this he described how such expansionism had come to dominate the thinking of the nationalist leaders of the region, including the comparatively reasonable Czech leaders:

> Of all the people whom we saw in the course of our journey, the Czechs seemed to have the most ability and common sense, the best organization, and the best leaders. They seem, however, to have been seized lately with a strong attack of imperialism, and a desire to dominate Central Europe. This was evident in frank conversations with President Masaryk; the Prime Minister, Dr. Kramar; and many others.[2]

The American Coolidge Mission, having visited most parts of East Central Europe in the winter of 1918 and the spring of 1919 in an attempt to study the economic conditions and the opposing wishes of the region's population, expressed similar views to the Peace Conference on its return.[3] Information gathered in this way was valued very highly on account of its freshness. [4] It is helpful to recall the words of József Eötvös, one of the greatest experts on nationalism and the nationality issue in the nineteenth century. These were written some seventy years before the period under discussion:

> Everywhere the struggle for equal rights continues; these have not been achieved, but everywhere there is a battle for control where there is no longer a need to fight against oppression.[5]

In handling such ambitions, the Great Powers were obliged to make choices regardless of their earlier decision to designate Poland, Romania, Czechoslovakia and Yugoslavia as "key" states. By standing up more for the idea of self-determination, they could have lent support to arrangements more closely in line with ethnic boundaries. Indeed, support for the self-determination principle was discernible in the policies they pursued. For example, David Lloyd George, the British prime minister, made serious efforts to block the transfer of a large German population to Poland (see the "Fontainebleau Memorandum" of March 25, 1919), and even achieved some success in the matter. Again, it was he who protested against the inclusion of large Hungarian populations in Czechoslovakia and Romania, although in these cases with much less ardor and fewer results. The working out of the "Curzon Line" also reflected the policies of moderation; according to this arrangement, Poland's eastern frontier would have followed more closely the lines of ethnic division between Poles, Ukrainians, and Byelorussians. But if stricter adherence to the self-determination principle was noticeable (primarily in British thinking, but occasionally also in Italian and American attitudes), it was later overshadowed. As the peace strategy demanded strong new states, the Principal Powers, nodding assent to economic and transportation arguments, generally supported the claims of the key states to important areas inhabited by other ethnic groups.

By way of compensation, the Principal Powers attached great significance to the protection of the larger minorities which now found themselves within the borders of the key states. Despite opposition from the latter, they insisted on legal guarantees for the protection of minorities. Thus, on the one hand, the Entente agreed to the augmentation of the new states at the expense of former enemies and Soviet Russia, but, on the other hand, wished to see the nationalities protected and their rights guaranteed under international law.

The United States, the British Empire, and France were united in their policy of minority protection as a result of carefully calculated political considerations. They were convinced that for the new states greater size and larger populations would represent greater strength only if the substantial minority populations thus incorporated were loyal to the sovereign power in the land. Otherwise, instead of promoting greater stability, the result would be the weakening of these states through dangerous internal strife. Thus, in order to facilitate consolidation, the Entente powers insisted—even in the face of opposition from the leaders of these new states—on internationally guaranteed protection for the minorities.

In the case of certain politicians, propaganda considerations may well have contributed to their lending support for minority protection. As counter-propaganda, minority protection could easily be employed against the self-determination principle or against the idea of deciding the fate of disputed areas by plebiscite. In other cases, humanitarian considerations may have explained the support given to minority protection. Basically, however, it was recognition of political realities, rather than the above, that motivated negotiations in this direction. The Principal Powers had valid political reasons for embarking on the course of internationally guaranteed minority protection. This seemed the only way to procure the minorities' loyalty to the new states and their trust in the durability of their protection—factors which would affect the consolidation of the new East Central European states.

Minority Protection in the Programs of the Entente Powers

Although each of the three Great Powers which were to attend the Peace Conference (the United States, the British Empire, and France) stood for minority protection, they did not support this policy with equal vigor. The United States was the main driving force behind the policy, with Britain following in second place. France went along with the policy; it was not a motivator, but neither was it a restraining force, as some earlier historians not yet fully acquainted with the sources mistakenly supposed. Next we shall examine the development of the American and French programs at the Peace Conference from the standpoint of minority protection.

The United States

The United States's initiatory role in the minority protection issue was determined by several factors, as we shall see later on. With the announcement of the Fourteen Points in January 1918, the United States assumed before the entire world the responsibility of providing a peace program. It was therefore confronted with the impending problems of the postwar re-alignment of states at a time when the war was still raging. At the outset this proved to be a decisive factor.

In his famous Fourteen Points speech on January 8, 1918, President Woodrow Wilson said nothing about minority protection. This was understandable given the circumstances and the immediate goal of the address. The war was still on, with serious dangers still in store for the Entente. Russia's departure from the alliance was only a matter of time: the Brest-Litovsk negotiations were already in progress. Germany was soon expected to move many more troops to the western front, with grave implications for the Allies. A program outlining the peace objectives was needed to strengthen the Allied resolve to continue with a hard and risky conflict. The American historian Victor S. Mamatey rightly points out that "the Fourteen Points was a liberal program but hardly an 'idealistic one.' It was intended less to provide a basis for peace than a justification for continuing war. In this immediate purpose it succeeded."[6] Moreover, President Wilson also had to take into account the ongoing secret negotiations on a possible Austro-Hungarian break with Germany.

In President Wilson's Fourteen Points, the right of nations to self-determination was singled out as the basic principle of the re-alignment. The consistent application of the principle in a region as ethnically diverse as East Central Europe could not, of course, have solved the minority problem—but would have mitigated it. Furthermore, in the original Fourteen Points the emergence of only one new national state, Poland, was envisaged in addition to certain frontier corrections in the Balkans in accordance with the national principle. There was nothing in the Fourteen Points indicating any intention to dismember Austria-Hungary. Thus, the authors of the scheme hoped to realize national self-determination in the "Danubian empire," ethnically the most heterogeneous region of East Central Europe, through a system providing local self-government on the American or the Swiss pattern within the context of a multinational and internally federalized, non-national state. The team entrusted with the task of drafting the Fourteen Points* realistically assessed the minority

---

* In September 1917, some months before announcing his famous Fourteen Points, Wilson asked Colonel House to set up a team of experts to work on the

problems likely to accompany a limited re-alignment of the type it predicted—very inaccurately as later events were to prove. It also raised the minority protection issue, albeit only in connection with a reconstituted Poland and an enlarged Romania.

The point of departure of the Inquiry team was that the protection of minorities was necessary in every "national" state inhabited by large national minorities where the character and the government of that state was defined by a single ethnic group differing from the others. In a multinational state where the state was not "national", this kind of minority protection was not required (the U.S.A. and Switzerland were regarded as such "non-national" states). The idea prevalent at the time was that —with the detachment of the regions inhabited by Poles, Romanians, Italians, and Serbs, and after certain internal reforms—the Austrian, Hungarian, Czech, Slovak, Croat, and Slovene populations in the parts of the Monarchy remaining could be organized into a similar non-national state. Since it was possible to redraw the frontiers of Finland and the Baltic States on the basis of the ethnic principle, the only two "national" states with large national minorities in the new East Central European system of states would be Poland and Romania.

In a draft copy of the Fourteen Points dated December 22, 1917 and handed to Wilson, the Inquiry team discussed in detail the chances of an independent Polish state. The draft concluded that, in order to survive, a new state between Germany and Russia would require internal stability, which, in view of such a state's ethnic composition, would only be possible through the development of democratic institutions.[7] Three months later, in a document dated March 20, 1918, the Inquiry commission again listed among the problems to be solved the "treatment of minorities"

---

formulation of peace objectives. The first task of the resulting body (which was known as the "American Commission of Inquiry for the Peace Conference," or "Inquiry" for short, and which had David Hunter Miller, Walter Lippmann and Dr. Mezes among its members) was the preparation of the Fourteen Points. A significant part of the "Inquiry" material was published (*Papers Relating to the Foreign Relations of the United States. The Paris Peace Conference 1919,* Washington, 1942–47, I, pp. 9–118). In late 1919 the "Inquiry" merged into the American peace delegation (the American Commission to Negotiate Peace).

in connection with Romania in particular and, more generally, "the guarantees of minority rights" throughout the region.[8]

It has already been said that at the time of the Inquiry commission's January and March reports or even at the time the Fourteen Points were published, the Monarchy was expected to survive, albeit reformed and smaller in size. It has also been stated that secret negotiations were taking place concurrently about a possible Austro-Hungarian break with Germany, and about the possibility of a separate peace treaty for the Monarchy. However, the events of spring 1918 made it clear that the Monarchy would be unable to leave the German alliance and that it would also be unable to implement the appropriate internal reforms.

By the early summer of 1918 the United States already expected the total disintegration of the Monarchy, and the formation of an independent Czechoslovakia and Yugoslavia. The Americans also anticipated the incorporation of large minorities in these two countries.

The protection of minorities, which had been under discussion in the United States' own peace commission since late 1917, was brought more into focus by the recognition of the Monarchy's impending collapse and the prospects of the formation of Czecho-Slovak and Yugoslav states. This was especially the case in October 1918, when the Central Powers' appeal for peace on the basis of the Fourteen Points arrived. It fell to Colonel House to inform the Allies of the revisions made in the United States' interpretation of the Fourteen Points. The ideas worked out by the Inquiry commission served as the basis for the revision. Especially significant were the modifications made to the tenth point, which now dealt with the disintegration of Austria-Hungary and the formation of states to replace it. In this point emphasis was laid on the importance of minority protection in Czechoslovakia, Yugoslavia, and Romania—the states to be built on the ruins of the Monarchy. In the words of the committee, "Transylvania... will undoubtedly join Romania, but provision must be made for the protection of the Magyars, Szeklers, and Germans who constitute a large minority."[9]

France[10]

The idea of minority protection was also incorporated into the French peace strategy, although the underlying concept was slightly different. In order to understand the French approach, we first need to make a slight detour and to study the contemporary French views on nationality and ethnicity.

The French placed great stress on the subjective element in the question of "nationality." For them, objective factors (for example, descent and language) were overshadowed by an individual's sentiments and choice: a French citizen who considered himself French—in other words who felt French and who had declared himself part of the French nation, was French, whatever his descent or first language. In general, the French view was that the reality behind claims to national sovereignty should be decided by means of plebiscites rather than by maps showing ethnicity. Accordingly, in regions where the national feeling and loyalty of the population were evident, such a plebiscite would not even be necessary.

This was also the concept behind the French argument on the question of Alsace-Lorraine: Alsace-Lorraine belonged to France, since its population—irrespective of the descent and the first language of the individuals living there—considered itself part of the French nation. The holding of a plebiscite on the issue was thought unnecessary by the French; in 1871 the German Empire had annexed these French provinces, and their reunion with France, on the basis of national self-determination, was a self-evident requirement.

There was nothing wrong with this nationality concept as long as the alien individuals or population, whether by descent or by language spoken, truly felt part of the majority nation. This aspect of the problem was also covered in the French concept: the verdict of the plebiscite, rather than some ethnic or linguistic map, was regarded as the crucial factor in areas where the situation was not clear-cut.

It would be wrong to conclude, however, that the French concept demanded that every border dispute should be settled by plebiscite. The above considerations constituted only one group of basic principles in the French peace plan. The other point to be considered concerned the possibilities of a country's economic viability. If the likely outcome of the plebiscite would be contrary to the fundamental political, that is to say economic, interests of the state concerned, then economic considerations should take precedence. Such an outcome, however, would create true "national minorities," in which case the rights of these minorities should be guaranteed before their integration into the majority nation was attempted. Between November 1918 and January 1919 (i.e. between the ending of the war and the opening of the Peace Conference), the French position received thorough elucidation in various statements, issued specifically for the purpose of reconciliation with the American team preparing for the Peace Conference. In a document drawn up on November 21, 1918, the dual nature of the French position received expression: "the right of peoples to decide their own destinies by free and secret ballot combined with the principle that the rights of minorities be guaranteed." The same idea was repeated in the program sent to the American team a week later: "free determination of the peoples combined with the rights of ethnic and religious minorities." In the draft program handed over to the Americans on January 5, 1919 the basic principle was again expressed: "public legislation ensuring the people the right of self-determination combined with the rights of ethnic and religious minorities."[11]

Essentially, the French position was that the new states would need to incorporate territories inhabited by national minorities: people who did not consider themselves part of the majority nation. Bearing in mind the interests, economic and otherwise, of the states concerned, there was simply no alternative. In such cases, however, the protection of the minorities guaranteed under international law would solve the problem. In other regions, where such economic considerations were not directly involved, plebiscites were called for.

Therefore, both the American and the French position was that the minorities would need to be protected. The difference lay elsewhere. In principle, the Americans accepted the creation of minorities only in the sense that they would live in a diaspora or be dispersed among the majority population, leaving them no alternative but the life of minorities.

By contrast, the French openly admitted that there could be

other ways of creating minorities in the process of re-aligning the states. This explains why, at least in the early stages, the United States placed special emphasis on the protection of Jewish minorities: their minority status was a given. In addition, the Americans spoke of inland pockets of minorities—the Szeklers and the Saxons in Transylvania, for example—and of mixed population areas. According to the American concept, therefore, everyone had the right to define his own state loyalties. This right, at least in principle, could not be curtailed. Quite naturally, however, there were minorities, either concentrated inside majority-populated territory or scattered among the majority people, which were unable to exercise this right. The French maintained that everyone had the right to define his or her own state loyalty or, if this were impossible, to be given minority protection. The issue as to which of these two considerations should be given priority in actual cases could be answered after studying the likely effects of the decision on the economic revival of the states concerned.

We should point out that in principle both the American and the French program stood for the protection of minorities. The differences concerned the ways in which the two parties conceived the creation of minorities and the range of people who would fall into this category. Later this difference of opinion became evident again when the American delegates to the Peace Conference were inclined to draw the frontiers closer to the lines of ethnic divisions than were their French counterparts. This was clearly illustrated in the first drafts of the border between Romania and Hungary. From the start, the French plans indicated frontiers very similar to those eventually adopted. The first American plan, by contrast, drew the border approximately half-way between historical Transylvania and the eventual frontier, following the ethnic division more closely.[12] In the turmoil of events, however, the American and the French plans moved closer and closer to one another, indicating that, despite theoretical differences, the French and the American positions could be reconciled in practice.

The Legal Precedents

An important factor in the formative planning of minority protection and the concomitant international guarantees was the fact that there were many nineteenth-century precedents in this area for linking the Great Powers' sanctioning of the formation of new states—or the expansion of existing ones—to obligations for the protection of minorities. Such linking was accepted in international law and was customary in the nineteenth century. Thus, the protection of minorities was regarded by the ruling élites of the leading powers neither as some kind of novelty, nor as something that would in any way restrict the sovereignty of the new state formations.

As regards religious minorities, protection guaranteed under international law went back several centuries, while the protection of national minorities under international law had a history of only 100 years. It was generally believed—on the basis of historical precedents—that when the leading powers granted international recognition to any new states, in other words when they sanctioned them, they were entitled to insist on certain preconditions. When they recognized and guaranteed a new state, they could not be indifferent to the internal affairs of the state, for which they, too, would bear responsibility. Thus the leading powers should be entitled to impose certain obligations on the new states in connection with the national minorities living there, and to place these obligations under international law and control.

The bibliography of historical and legal-historical literature concerning such legal precedents is long.[13] The study of individual cases would require more space than is available, yet those nineteenth-century precedents, to which references were repeatedly made during the drafting of the minority protection accords of the Peace Conference, need to be discussed. Such references were even included among the most significant documents of the Peace Conference. In this respect the three most important historical precedents of the nineteenth century were as follows: 1. the decisions of the Congress of Vienna of 1815 concerning Poland's division into three parts; 2. the minority protection clauses signed first in 1830 at the birth of an independent Greek state, and then in 1863, at the time of its later expansion; and, above all, 3. the similar work of the Congress of Berlin in 1878.

The first internationally-guaranteed minority protection accord concerning national, as opposed to religious, minorities dealt with the Polish problem at the Congress of Vienna held after the defeat of Napoleon. The Congress nullified the changes introduced by Napoleon, and reinstated the division of the Polish people under the rule of the tsar, the Habsburgs, and the Hohenzollerns. At the same time, it noted the nationality rights of the Polish minorities in an international agreement.

At the Congress of Vienna, Britain proposed that the emperors who had Polish subjects should sign bilateral agreements with one another, in which they would undertake obligations enabling their Polish subjects to preserve their national identity. In May 1815 bilateral agreements were signed between Russia and Austria and between Russia and Prussia in which these powers promised to provide national institutions for their Polish subjects. On June 9, in the first paragraph of the final document signed by the eight powers participating at the Congress (Britain, Spain, France, Austria, Portugal, Prussia, Russia, and Sweden) it was stated that the Poles were to be given national representation and institutions in all three empires. On the basis of this agreement, the Polish national minorities gained autonomy (although not in equal measure) in all three states.[14]

The possible sanctions to be faced by a signatory power in the event of non-compliance with the agreement were not stipulated by the Congress, nor were they set down in any subsequent document. However, intervention in such cases was considered justified. In 1831, when Russia abolished autonomy in retaliation for the Polish insurrection, the French government protested through its ambassador to St. Petersburg—with the result that autonomy was restored. In 1863, following a second revolt, the governments of Britain and Austria intervened, referring to the 1815 agreement and pointing out that not even another uprising could relieve the tsarist government of its obligation to grant autonomy to the Poles. The British and Austrian governments wanted to call an international conference on the issue, but Prince Aleksandr Gorchakov, the Russian foreign minister, rejected the appeal—although without denying his country's obligations under the agreement or the right of Britain and Austria to intervene. Gorchakov argued that it was up to the signatory powers to determine how they fulfilled their obligations; nevertheless, Polish autonomy within the Russian Empire was restored shortly afterwards.

Thus, the accord signed in 1815 concerning the right of Polish autonomy in all three empires was an obligation, the observance of which was monitored with interest even before World War I, both by the outsider states (primarily Britain) and by the powers directly involved. Neither the international obligation nor the right of intervention was ever called into question. And although a whole century passed between the Congress of Vienna and the Paris Peace Conference, the problem was still very much alive, especially since the 1815 Congress of Vienna was, in more ways than one (procedural issues, etc.), still regarded as a precedent by the participants in the Paris Peace Conference.

The other legal precedent often brought up during the Peace Conference was associated with Greek independence, established in 1830. All the previous interventions by the Great Powers in Turkey's affairs had been in support of the Christian population living under Turkish rule. In agreements concluded with the (already declining) Turkish Empire there had been references to minority protection even as early as the seventeenth and the eighteenth centuries. It must be pointed out, however, that although these endeavors belonged to the protection of religious minorities in the Balkans, where the formation of states had been based mostly on religious divisions, by the nineteenth century they basically meant the protection of a "national" character. As well as constituting religious minorities, the Christian populations living in European Turkey (for example, the Greeks, the Bulgarians, and the Romanians) also formed ethnic and national groups distinct from the Turks.

Thus, the protection of the Christian population within the Turkish Empire constituted a centuries-old practice. With the declaration of independence in Greece, the situation was reversed for the first time. In this case the Moslem (in other words, the Turkish) population became a religious (or national) minority, with the Catholic population constituting the other religious minority as opposed to the Greek Orthodox majority.

On February 3, 1830, after Greek independence had been established with the help of the Western powers, Britain, France, and Russia signed an agreement and published its content (Greece was not among the signatories). In this statement they guaranteed the sovereignty of the new and independent Greece, requiring that in order to preserve the new state from

> the calamities which the rivalries of the religions therein professed might excite, agree that all the subjects of the new state, whatever their religion may be, shall be admissible to all public employments, functions and honors, and be treated on a footing of perfect equality, without regard to difference of creed, in their relations, religious, civil or political.[15]

A similar agreement and statement followed the change of dynasty in 1863, when the Ionian Islands, formerly a British protectorate, were ceded to the Kingdom of Greece.

The significance of the minority protection agreements accompanying the establishment of Greek independence spread beyond the country's borders, as these treaties set the pattern for further agreements and statements which followed the liberation of other Balkan peoples from Ottoman rule. In these agreements the Great Powers promised acknowledgment of sovereignty in return for obligations undertaken by the state in question for the protection of minorities. Precisely the same happened after the Crimean War, when in 1856 self-governing Moldavia and Wallachia (which officially were still under Turkish sovereignty) were recognized by the leading powers:

> All religions and those who profess them shall enjoy equal liberty and equal protection in the two principalities... All classes of the population, without any distinction of birth or religion, shall enjoy equality of civil rights and in particular the right of property in all its forms.

These passages were primarily intended to protect the Jewish communities living within the borders of the two principalities, as the number of Moslems and Catholics in the region was very small.[16]

The third legal precedent persistently referred to throughout the Paris Peace Conference was the resolution adopted by the Congress of Berlin in 1878. The problems concerning the religious and national minorities of the Balkan states were discussed in great detail by the statesmen assembled there. In a document containing several articles, the Congress passed a resolution laying down specific rules for each of the states concerned. It recognized the states of Serbia, Romania and Montenegro, which had all cast off the last vestiges of Turkish sovereignty, and the state of Bulgaria, still a Turkish protectorate. The recognition was made dependent on these states guaranteeing the freedom of every citizen (and visitor) to profess his or her religion. Another demand was that all subjects, regardless of religion, should enjoy equal civil and political rights and should be eligible for all public posts, as well as for every profession and trade. Compliance with all these rules was regarded as a necessary precondition for recognition. Only when the new, independent states accepted and satisfied these conditions did the Great Powers recognize them.

The recognition of Romania was delayed because of the insistence of Germany, Britain, France, and Italy that Article 7 of the Romanian constitution be modified. This article originally said that only Christians were eligible for Romanian citizenship, which, in the view of these four powers contradicted the Congress's resolution.

References to this resolution were made during the period between the closing of the Congress and World War I whenever the Great Powers intervened in the affairs of other states. As a result, the legalistic approach was still very much alive at the time when the Paris Peace Conference was convened. Most importantly, it was accepted practice that the recognition of new or enlarged states was accompanied by the settling of minority problems within those states to the satisfaction of the leading Western powers.

Thus, these precedents were not only known to a small circle of judiciary experts, but also represented currently accepted standards in international politics at the time of the Paris Peace Conference.

The League of Nations Covenant and the Protection of Minorities

In the months following the end of World War I, the new states of Central and East Europe were established on a *de facto* footing. The process was still continuing in January 1919, when the Peace Conference convened, and ended in some areas only after the first phase of the Conference. The accompanying events, which involved heavy fighting and violent animosity, made it clear to the leaders of the three Principal Powers that, in the interests of regional stability, there would be an urgent need for international guarantees of the minority protection measures contemplated earlier.

The specific problem of minority protection and the relevant international guarantees first arose in connection with the establishment of the League of Nations. The Conference gave priority to discussions relating to the League of Nations, and formed a committee, to be chaired by President Wilson, to work out its Covenant.

The League of Nations, an organization to preserve peace and prevent another war, was not solely Wilson's idea, but originated in various objectives. For example, on June 5, 1917 the lower house of the French parliament, by an overwhelming majority, passed the following resolution: "The Chamber trusts that the efforts of the Army of the Republic and Allies will permit, after Prussian militarism is overthrown, the securing of lasting guarantees of peace and independence for great and small nations alike by association in a League of Nations, already in preparation."[17]

In the neutral countries, similar suggestions were made by groups of educated people, and in some cases societies were formed to promote the idea. Among the first such societies was the *Organization Centrale pour une Paix Durable,* founded in The Hague in 1915. This not only pressed for the foundation of an international body to safeguard peace, but also argued for the protection of national minorities within a stable system of states in Europe, in the interests of eliminating the causes of war.[18]

The efforts to found a League of Nations were also backed by the governments of the Entente powers, but the most forthright supporter of the idea during the last year of the war was undoubtedly President Wilson. The fact that he reserved the last point in his fourteen-point program for mention of a League of Nations indicates the importance he attached to it. Nevertheless, the first actual plan for such a body was drawn up by the Phillimore Committee, the British counterpart of the American Inquiry commission. The committee, which was set up by the British government in January 1917 and headed by Lord Phillimore, did not, in the end, work together with the Inquiry team, although the British proposed this in February 1918.[19] The Phillimore Committee completed its own draft plan for the establishment of a League of Nations on March 20, 1918.

It was also in early 1917 that the French government set up its own committee, chaired by Léon Bourgeois, to develop the concept of an international organization to be established after the war. Its work was completed on June 8, 1918 and its proposals promptly communicated to London. The British government passed them on to the Phillimore Committee, whose own report was sent to Foreign Secretary Arthur J. Balfour on August 9. In the view of the Phillimore Committee, the British and the French positions were compatible.[20]

The British and the French drafts were both officially forwarded to President Wilson and were known to the leading members of the American administration.[21] It was after consideration of the British and the French proposals that the first concrete American draft, a document of twenty-three paragraphs which also incorporated the recommendations of the Inquiry commission, was completed and handed over for Wilson's approval in July 1918. Neither this document, nor the plans of the British and the French committees said anything about minority protection. Wilson linked the guaranteeing of the new status quo to the possibility of altering it later by peaceful means. The basic idea was that the new states would be formed more or less on the basis of self-determination, but that peaceful ways had to be left open for future modifications should the need arise. This approach did not require minority protection, and Wilson's draft proposals for a League of Nations, proposals which were complete by the time he left for Europe, were framed accordingly.

In January 1919, Wilson, already in Paris, produced a new version of his proposals, now paying particular heed to Miller's advice. In the so-called "First Paris Draft" less room was given for possible future alterations, while the protection of minorities was mentioned in the sixth paragraph: "The League of Nations shall require all new States to bind themselves as a condition precedent to their recognition as independent or autonomous States, to accord to all racial or national minorities within their several jurisdictions exactly the same treatment and security, both in law and in fact, that is accorded to the racial or national majority of their people." That very same month, he widened the scope of the proposal to include the religious minorities, too.

Wilson's new drafts also contained the idea that the League of Nations would guarantee the frontiers of member-states, along with the pledge (now a little less definite) that the possibility of peaceful border corrections under League supervision would be left open. In Wilson's view it was important that the joint Anglo-American proposal be available to the committee before it began work on the Covenant of the League. The British view regarding the incorporation of the minority protection in the Covenant was, however, at odds with that held by the Americans. On the part of the British, a detailed proposal was put together by General Jan C. Smuts, and a shorter one by Lord Robert Cecil.[22] Both plans were sent to the Americans on January 1; neither said anything about the protection of minorities.[23]

To iron out the differences, talks were held between Miller and Lord Cecil in January 1919.[24] The British considered Wilson's proposed minority protection measures too general, and in view of the fact that the minority situation varied enormously from one country to the next, wished to lay down specific rules for each state in separate agreements. And since the formation of the new states was still under way at the time, the British suggested that the problem should be left out of the Covenant of the League.

The talks continued at a higher level on January 31, this time attended by Wilson and Colonel Edward M. House on the American side and by General Smuts and Lord Cecil on the British.[25] After the adoption of the British view on the minority protection issue, Miller and House were entrusted with the wording of the joint proposal, which was completed on February 2.[26] The committee headed by Wilson started to work out the Covenant of the League on February 3.

Eventually, the Covenant of the League of Nations came to be based on the joint Anglo-American proposal, which the French and the Italian delegations also accepted. The sanctity of borders was guaranteed in the strongest terms:

> The members of the League undertake to respect and preserve against external aggression the territorial integrity and existing political independence of all members of the League (Article 10).

At the same time, the possibility of future border corrections was hinted at in very vague form:

> The Assembly may from time to time advise the reconsideration by Members of the League of treaties which have become inapplicable and the consideration of international conditions whose continuance might endanger the peace of the world (Article 19).

No obligation relating to minority protection was included in the Covenant, though Articles 11, 12, and 13 were formulated to leave open the possibility for the inclusion of minority protection in later international agreements. Thus, Article 11, Paragraph 2 states:

> It is also declared to be the friendly right of each Member of the League to bring to the attention of the Assembly or of the Council any circumstance whatever affecting international relations which threatens to disturb international peace or the good understanding between nations upon which peace depends.

Since the Principal Powers, who created the League of Nations, regarded the minority question from the very outset as a problem that might disturb peace and "good understanding between nations," Article 11 provided the basis for placing this whole issue under the aegis of the League. Articles 12 and 13 expressed the possibility of, or need for, a decision by an elected court of arbitration, which also assumed significance with regard to minority affairs.

Thus the omission of minority protection from the Covenant of the League of Nations did not mean the downgrading of the problem; on the contrary, the issue was no longer treated in terms of generalized formulae but in conformity with historical precedent, setting concrete obligations for the new states.

The Representation of Minorities at the Conference: the Jewish Organizations

Albeit unofficially, the minorities were represented at the Peace Conference through organizations protecting the interests of East-European Jewry. These organizations enjoyed good relations with the influential circles of the Entente powers.

There were Jewish organizations based in the United States and Britain which lent support to the nationality-type Jewish communities of Eastern Europe. Persistent lobbying by these organizations played a significant part in the decision of the Principal Powers, most notably of the United States and Britain, to incorporate minority protection in their respective peace programs. Given the circumstances, effective representation of minority rights at the Peace Conference, actively involving the minorities themselves, was not possible in any other way. Every subject or minority nationality of the old East Central Europe unequivocally stood for the inclusion of its people in an independent state of its own. Unfortunately, the former subject nationalities, which were all majority nationalities under the new arrangement and which enjoyed the status of "winners," were no longer interested in the protection of minorities. As for the new minorities, they were either regarded as "enemies" (the Germans, Hungarians, Bulgarians, and Turks) not even represented at the Conference, or suffered the consequences of being associated with revolutionary Russia (the Russians, Byelorussians, and Ukrainians). Thus, for many minorities of Eastern Europe the Jewish organizations meant the only prospect of representation at the Conference.

Sizeable Jewish communities exhibiting nationality characteristics could be found in Poland, the eastern parts of Czechoslovakia, and in Romania. The organizations representing these communities were able to send delegates to Paris. These organizations and the American Jewish Committee formed a joint group, called the *Comité des Delegations Juives*. In early April, the new group established contact with Miller, the minorities expert in the United States delegation. This contact developed into a lasting link and provided the "channel" through which the *Comité*'s requests and program could effectively be communicated to the Conference. There were Jewish organizations based in Britain and France whose representatives did not agree with the *Comité*'s policies on cultural autonomy and which therefore refused to participate in its work. These represented the assimilated Jewry of Western Europe and claimed for the Jews of Eastern Europe only those rights which they themselves possessed: complete and all-embracing civic equality. The *Comité* went beyond this and, in addition to such basic rights, also demanded cultural autonomy.

Although the *Comité* initially served to represent those Jewish communities of Eastern Europe which possessed the characteristics of nationalities, it soon came to speak out for the protection of all the region's national minorities; in order to solve the problem, the *Comité* recommended that the Conference establish cultural autonomy for each such nationality. In a study written after World War II, a German historian remarked:

In Paris, it was primarily the representatives of the Jewish minorities who were able to influence the decisions concerning the regulation of the minority problems. But without the support of American Jewry, which backed the East-European concept of minority protection, they would not have succeeded in influencing those decisions.[27]

In 1938, Zoltán Baranyai arrived at similar conclusions in an article written for the journal *Magyar Szemle*:

Clearly, the Jews, and especially their delegation to Paris, deserve much credit for making the idea of minority protection acceptable to the Council, to the extent that the latter ordered the Committee to work out the Minority Accords. By continually supplying information, the Jewish minority experts provided the arguments and the material for those who, against steady opposition from Brătianu, Paderewski and Pašić, were convinced that a certain amount of protection for the minorities was definitely necessary, and who continued to stand by their conviction.[28]

The Contemporary View on Minority Rights

Before launching into a study of the historic development of minority protection legislation at the Peace Conference, an examination of the most important approaches to minority rights seems appropriate. Rather than study the actual rights enjoyed by minorities in the particular historical period when the Peace Conference was sitting, in this chapter we intend to investigate the major ideas, concepts and developments in this regard, with emphasis on the practical side.

The study of legal interpretation and political practice at this time is a task verging on the impossible, especially when confined to a short survey. The reason for this is the bewildering diversity of contemporary views on the subject: the various nationalities had very different ideas on what rights to demand for themselves, and contrary opinions on the issue even existed among members of the same nationality. Also, members of the same nationality in two different countries might express different positions and demands. Moreover, the leading politicians and political theorists in the various states also had greatly divergent thoughts concerning national minorities. Again, in this respect one must consider not only the different ideas of the politicians in power, but also the various approaches to minority rights existing in each state.

In spite of the diversity concerning the issue, the concepts and the practical propositions can be grouped into three main categories, although many approaches and concepts can best be described as combining various elements of these categories. Also, as we shall see later on, this threefold division of the problem exhibits a certain hierarchy.

The Equality of Civil Rights

The point of departure, or the minimum (but often sufficient) demand, in the formulation of minority rights was always the requirement that members of a minority (that is to say, people different from the majority population in language, descent, race, or religion) should enjoy exactly the same civil rights as any other citizen of the state. In the course of the nineteenth century the modern bourgeois constitutional states based on the liberal principles of "liberty, equality, and fraternity" gradually came to admit the equality of civil rights, in theory if not always in practice. Earlier distinctions, which were fundamental to the feudal legal system and philosophy, were accordingly eliminated, with the result that some "minority" problems were automatically resolved or at least provided with some basis for settlement.

In the nineteenth century, several minority problems achieved solution within those liberal democracies which provided true equality before the law without the need for additional legal measures.

Those members of a minority population who assimilated encountered no more legal obstacles, with the result that their "minority" demands were met. Those minorities wanting to preserve their identity (their language, culture, religion, etc.) but not striving for autonomy or a state of their own (either because of their small population or for historical reasons) were able to maintain and develop their communities and to achieve integration into the state by exercising the right to free association guaranteed in all liberal states. However, this process was not always without its problems. In countries where the state was not explicitly national (in the sense of multi-ethnic), the integration of minorities, if the state were liberal, thus guaranteeing civic equality including the right of free association to its citizens, proceeded more smoothly than in decidedly national states, such as France. Nevertheless, in these European states also, minority problems were more or less settled on the basis of civil rights and free association, without the need to introduce any further legal regulations or separate minority protection.

When discussing minority issues at the Paris Peace Conference, the statesmen of the Principal Powers relied primarily on domestic experience. Theirs were precisely those countries in which equality of civil rights had proved adequate in solving the minority problem. Interestingly, in these countries only rarely did minorities require additional rights; France's Catalan population was an exception in this respect. (The Irish question did not at the time constitute a minority problem, as in this case the conflict was between two countries.) One should also remember that the black minority's movement in the United States was fighting for the rights of black *individuals,* to achieve rights guaranteed in the Constitution, but often withheld in everyday life. In fact, America's black population strongly protested against being regarded as a minority to be distinguished from the majority.

To give a rather general summary, it can be argued that the minority issue at the Paris Peace Conference was dominated by the experiences of the prominent Western leaders which were rooted in the more advanced civic structures of their own countries.

In East Central Europe, in the nineteenth century and at the turn of the twentieth century, there prevailed a different approach to the problem—both among top government officials and within the minorities themselves. In this region, equality of civil rights alone seemed insufficient to resolve the problem. This constituted a realistic appraisal of the situation, considering that here the national minorities constituted substantial national "blocs"—to the extent that in two of the countries, Austria and Hungary, the "majority" nations were, in fact, minorities.

The Hungarian view of law and the Hungarian concept of nation closely followed the Western European models. However, if one considers Hungary's ethnic composition, as well as its national composition and historical development, this in itself could never be enough to solve the minority problem.

The Nationalities Law of 1868[29] started out from the principle of the equality of civil rights; in its preamble it emphatically declared "all citizens, regardless of nationality" to be "equal members of the community," comprising "one nation in the political sense." Since in Hungary the law did not recognize nationality *communities* within the "indivisible and unitary Hungarian nation," but did recognize *individuals* whose first language or declared nationality was not Hungarian, additional legislation to regulate the use of languages seemed necessary. Such legislation was extended to cover a wide area, including the right to receive elementary education in one's mother-tongue—a concession the state was obliged to take into account when developing its system of schools (Articles 17-19).

But although the law did not explicitly recognize the communal rights of national minorities, it did leave open the possibility for them to establish their own schools and to develop their own cultures. Consequently, certain pointers towards cultural autonomy could be discovered in Hungarian legislation, despite the fact that the equal civil rights of the *individuals* formed the legal basis for handling the minority question:

As before, in future every citizen regardless of his nationality status, just as every village, Church and parish, will continue to enjoy the right, either individually or by joining forces with others, to establish institutions of elementary, secondary, or higher education. For this purpose, and also for the establishment of institutions to advance their language, the arts, the sciences, agriculture, industry and commerce, citizens will be permitted, under the legally regulated supervision by the state, to form associations and societies, to lay down the rules for their unions and societies, to act in accordance with the rules approved by the government, to raise funds, and, under government supervision, to manage these funds in line with the lawful demands of their nationality. The educational and other institutions thus established—in the case of the schools, without abridging the regulations of the Public Education Act—are to be treated on an equal footing with the state-governed institutions of the same character and level. The languages used in private institutions and associations are to be determined by the founders (Article 26).

We would digress too far if we were to investigate the reasons why this liberal-minded endeavor—which was in line with Western European thinking and which contained elements pointing towards cultural autonomy—met with failure. Nevertheless, it must be said that this failure could not be explained merely by the inconsistencies in the law's application, inconsistencies which had deeper roots. France constituted a "national" state, which seemed reasonable since only 5—6 percent of its population fell into a minority category, with an overwhelming majority choosing the path of assimilation. In this case, therefore, the national state was able to solve most of its minority problems simply by guaranteeing the equality of civil rights.

In the United States and Great Britain, although not as centralized nor ethnically "pure" as France, the enactment of equal civil rights was also sufficient, despite their heterogeneous ethnic composition, to resolve the issue. The freedom to form autonomous organizations, a federal structure, and equality of civil rights were adequate in themselves in pointing towards a satisfactory outcome of the minority question. But Hungary's ethnic structure did not suit the legal and the organizational concept of the "national state"; and the equality of civil rights, even when supplemented with elements of cultural autonomy, was therefore not enough to bring a lasting solution to the minority issue. Fundamentally, equality of civil rights was the correct approach to nationality problems, but the legal and organizational structure of a "national state" could not solve the problems of the nationality composition which existed. The equality of civil rights, even when augmented with elements of cultural autonomy, was no substitute for recognition of a country's multinational character and the establishment of a federal structure.

Cultural Autonomy

In East Central Europe, too, those who contemplated the granting of minority rights regarded equality of civil rights as the first step. However, only rarely did they believe that this was sufficient, taking the view that the minorities also had the right to autonomous management of their own cultural affairs (including their language and network of schools).

The concept of cultural autonomy was devised on Austrian territory. It was advocated in its advanced form by the Austrian Social Democrats at the turn of the century, and was based primarily on the thinking of Karl Renner, although the basic idea had already been incorporated in the draft Kremsier constitution of 1849 and in the constitution of December 1867. As we have already seen, certain elements of it were also incorporated in the Hungarian Nationalities Law of 1868.

The December 1867 Austrian constitution, which was based on the draft constitution of 1849, declared the equality of the nationalities within the state, together with their right to foster their own languages and to preserve their national identities (*Reichsgesetzblatt,* 1867, Nr. 124. Paragraph 19). As opposed to the Hungarian constitution where the subject of the law was the individual citizen, in Austrian lands a community was recognized as a collective legal entity, even when its rights recorded in the legal code merely extended to the development of its culture and language. The law declared the various national and ethnic groups (the term *Volksstamm* was used in the Austrian law) to be equal, but their rights were restricted to the cultivation of their language and national identity, and there was no mention of sovereignty. Recognition of the nationalities' "cultural autonomy" was implicitly contained in this concept, but so was denial of the right to territorial autonomy. In the contemporary Austrian interpretation of constitutional law, the state was considered to be non-national, or "supra-national," since the realm of "national" was manifested in language and specific national culture, while the state domain, indifferent to the national idea, was "above" all this.

The long-term policies of the national movements everywhere included the demand for political and constitutional organization on a territorial basis. Even when the territorial autonomy envisaged fell short of an *independent* state, it was nevertheless sovereignty that was demanded. Not even the Austrian concept extended quite as far as this, although the Austrian legal approach admitted and codified the collective and autonomous character of the nationalities in the sphere of language, schooling, and national culture, preparing the ground for concepts aiming to realize the rights of the national minorities within the framework of cultural autonomy.

Cultural autonomy, predominantly in cases where the national minorities lived thinly dispersed over wide areas or in small, closed communities, often proved a useful starting point for settling the minority question. At the turn of the century, however, such an arrangement could not have brought a comprehensive and general solution to the Austrian minority problem. Nevertheless, credit must be given to the Austrian Social Democrats for comprehensively working out this particular minority approach regardless of the fact that the national movements in Austria were going in a direction which made a federal arrangement based on territorial autonomies the only plausible solution.

Oszkár Jászi's contemporary criticism of Karl Renner's scheme, which the future Austrian president had summarized immediately prior to the disintegration of Austria-Hungary (in his work *Das Selbstbestimmungsrecht der Nationen in besonderer Anwendung auf Österreich,* Leipzig–Wien, 1918), was justified. Jászi wrote: "Intentionally or otherwise, the nationalities are denied the right of territorial autonomy in Renner's proposal also." He continued:

> Renner also seems to forget that one of the most striking aspects of our current democratic endeavors is precisely the creation of an increasingly elaborate system of territorial autonomies... In situations where we are facing sincere determination to achieve national sovereignty, the granting of narrowly-interpreted nationality demands is not enough.[30]

Jászi's criticism of Renner's "meanness" towards Austria's national minorities was warranted. But he himself was no less "mean"—at least before the autumn of 1918—to the national minorities in Hungary. With the exception of the Croat demands, Jászi saw no justification for the national minorities' claims to territorial autonomy. At the same time, however, he supported the nationalities in their struggle for school systems of their own and for the right to cultivate their own cultures, courageously standing up for these views against the authorities.

Territorial Autonomy

In his book quoted above, as well as in his earlier writings, Oszkár Jászi was essentially correct to distinguish between nationality movements (which for various reasons—for example, unsuitable geographical location, or small or thinly-dispersed population—would have been happy with and ready to accept cultural autonomy) and national movements whose struggle for sovereignty had real prospects.

All the major national movements of the more advanced kind were moving towards demands for sovereignty. Nevertheless, for this there were economic, historical, and foreign policy preconditions which these movements could not overlook. Naturally, not every movement with a tendency towards sovereignty reached the point of actually demanding it; indeed the programs were not necessarily oriented towards the maximum demand. Federation or territorial autonomy within another state were also regarded as possible solutions. Therefore, the national movements which ended up demanding sovereignty often settled for territorial autonomy of some sort, although the resulting arrangements did not always prove lasting.

During the last few decades before World War I, there were numerous attempts to solve the national minorities problem in East Central Europe by the granting of territorial autonomy. Finland and Congress Poland had both enjoyed territorial autonomy within the Russian Empire. The dualist state of Austria-Hungary could itself be regarded as a special type of federation. At the same time, Croatia within Hungary and Galicia within Austria both possessed territorial autonomy of considerable breadth. It would have been to the advantage of the region if the list had been longer.

The sovereignty of those nationalities possessing territorial autonomy was somewhat limited by the central government and, consequently, such an arrangement was often considered unsatisfactory by the nationalities themselves. Efforts were continually made to extend this autonomy, and competition between the various elements in the federation was a source of constant strife. Nevertheless, for every national minority which could not aspire to separate statehood, territorial autonomy remained the highest attainable form of self-government.

Chapter 3
The Drafting of the Minority Protection Treaties
The Creation of the Commission on New States and Minorities

On April 28, 1919, a plenary session of the Peace Conference endorsed the report of the committee headed by President Wilson. (This committee had been formed on January 25 to prepare the draft proposal of the Covenant of the League of Nations.) By that time, helped by the work of the various committees set up by the Conference, the Supreme Council had prepared the draft of the German peace treaty, which was handed a few days later (on May 7, during another plenary session) to representatives of the German government.

Committee IX, dealing with territorial questions, had decided the basic outlines of its position concerning the boundaries of the new and enlarged states, and had submitted the problems to the Supreme Council for study. Since it had been agreed that, in deciding the borders for these states, it was not the principles of ethnicity (or self-determination), but economic, transport, and strategic considerations that would be the main criteria, the positions adopted over the matter of boundaries indicated that there would be large national minorities within the new states. It therefore became a matter of urgency to work out a draft for making the protection of minorities an obligation of the new and enlarged states.

At the May 1 meeting of the Supreme Council—by then it had become known as the Council of Four, although after April 24, when Orlando indignantly left for home, it functioned briefly as the Council of Three—Wilson proposed the working out of the minority protection obligations. On the same day Wilson and Lloyd George delegated to the committee David Hunter Miller and James W. Headlam-Morley respectively. Prime Minister Georges Clemenceau delegated Philippe Berthelot, who then became its chairman. The committee, which was officially known as the

Commission on New States and Minorities, was later joined by an Italian delegate and a Japanese delegate.[1]

At the May 1 session of the Council of Four, as at its other meetings, no exact minutes were taken. The fullest account of the meeting is given in the relevant American publication of the 1940s,[2] although this leaves many gaps. Some of the missing information was supplied by the notes published in the 1950s by Paul Mantoux, the chief interpreter.[3] There remains, however, an important question on which these sources are not clear, namely the Council of Four's instructions regarding the principles that were to guide the actions of the committee. Probably, the instructions themselves were not yet final or unequivocal on this point.

From the American Papers it becomes apparent that the minority sections of Wilson's earlier draft plans prepared for the League of Nations, as well as Miller's notes—in line with the April 29 draft by the *Comité des Delegations Juives* and expressing a desire for cultural autonomy—were recommended to the committee. On the other hand, Mantoux's notes reveal that any proposal for minority autonomy met with opposition, because it would mean "a state within a state." It is not clear, however, whether only comprehensive political-regional autonomy was rejected here, but looser forms of autonomy as well. Even less clear was the attitude toward the concept of cultural autonomy and its various forms of implementation.

At the first meeting of the committee on May 2, when only the representatives of the United States and Britain participated, the decision was taken—possibly on the basis of the guidance given by the Council of Four—that its work should not aim at the establishment of corporate cultural autonomy. This did not mean, however, that all forms of cultural autonomy were to be excluded. It was on the basis of this decision that the first draft outline of Poland's minority protection obligations was prepared.

Now the immediate problem was to decide which minority protection clauses should be included in the German peace treaty, as the draft of the treaty was to be handed to the German delegation within a few days. There was insufficient time to incorporate Poland's minority protection obligations into the German peace treaty, but the committee felt that a reference to these obligations in one of the paragraphs was definitely in order.

By this time it had become clear that, unlike the situation along Germany's western and northern borders where (excluding the return of Alsace and Lorraine to France) only minor corrections in favor of Belgium and Denmark were planned, in the east the redrawing of Germany's frontiers would necessarily involve the assignment to Poland of large German populations in the regions of Posen, Silesia, West Prussia, and East Prussia—regardless of the outcome of plebiscites which might have to be held in some of these areas.

The committee's proposal was discussed by the Council of Four on May 3; the Council basically accepted the draft of the Polish treaty and instructed the committee to continue its work. It also approved the proposal that the German peace treaty should contain only a reference to the Principal Powers' intention to conclude an agreement with Poland which would obligate that country to protect its minorities, and Poland's preliminary consent was obtained for this move.[4] Accordingly, the foundations were laid for Article 93 of the German peace treaty which stated that the Principal Powers and Poland would sign a pact "to protect the interests of those inhabitants of Poland who differ from the majority population in race, language, or religion."

It is worth noting that the insertion of a similar article in relation to Czechoslovakia was not originally intended. The explanation for this lies in the fact that the German population now belonging to Czechoslovakia had formerly belonged to Austria; consequently, the reference to its protection was to be included in Austria's peace treaty. However, after the disintegration of the Monarchy, the sympathy of the German population of Bohemia, and especially the sympathy of the Sudeten Germans, whose territory bordered on Germany, was not with Austria, but with Germany, where public opinion reciprocated such feelings.

Reacting to the terms of peace transmitted on May 7, the German reply note requested that the articles should not mention the protection of minority interests in Poland in general terms only, but that explicit reference should be made to specific minority protection measures. Later, the reply note of May 29 requested reference to the establishment of "cultural autonomy" in even more definite terms: "It would be well if a still more complete cultural autonomy could be procured, on the basis of national land registers. For her part, Germany is determined to treat foreign minorities within her territory according to the same principles."[5] These demands were rejected,[6] reflecting the Council of Four's original May 1 position restricting or rejecting autonomy. On the other hand, the German peace treaty did eventually include a passage on the minority protection obligations of Czechoslovakia (Article 86), formulated in a way similar to the text of the article referring to Poland's obligations.[7]

The *Comité des Delegations Juives,* which specifically represented the Jewish minorities, but which on the more general level also voiced the demands of all the minorities of the region, joined the Germans in calling for cultural autonomy for the minorities. On May 15, on the same day the German requests were submitted, the *Comité* handed to the American delegation its last memorandum on the subject. This was also rejected. The most prominent leaders of the *Comité,* the Americans Mack and Marshall, responded by leaving Paris immediately. Miller did likewise in late May. He supported the idea both in the United States delegation and in the Commission on New States and Minorities of settling the minority problem by establishing cultural autonomies. However, this disagreement between the American delegation and the Jewish organizations on the goals to be pursued did not mean a breakdown of relations between them; in his summary report compiled for Wilson, Colonel House stated: "The United States is particularly interested in the protection of minorities..., more especially in the protection of the Jews in Poland and Roumania."[8]

Thus, with the creation of the Commission on New States and Minorities, the preparations for minority protection proceeded in definite steps, such as the wording of clauses for the German peace treaty and the drafting of the Polish treaty. However, they did not progress towards guaranteeing autonomy, but towards acceptance and reinforcement of the "national" character of the new and enlarged—in reality, multinational—states. They also moved towards assuring equal rights for the minorities in all fields, recognizing their specific interests in schooling, cultural needs, and use of their mother-tongue, but rejecting their emergence as political bodies within the state structure. In this way, international minority protection shifted in the direction of guarantees for minimal minority rights within the framework of basic human freedoms. This tendency did not exclude from the international protection of minorities the inclusion within the obligations of certain elements of collective rights and cultural autonomy. Still less did it limit those states containing minority populations in settling minority problems within a framework which covered more than just internationally-protected minority rights, in the interests of the states' internal stability and the nationalities' integration. Such settlements were firmly demanded, and were even implemented, in Finland, Czechoslovakia, and Estonia.

After the Council of Four had approved, at its May 1 and May 3 sessions, the clauses on minority protection to be included in the German peace treaty and had determined the main line of the minority protection accord to be concluded with Poland, on May 6 it instructed the committee to draw up the Polish treaty in full and to begin wording the treaties to be concluded with the other new states, Czechoslovakia and Yugoslavia. The Council of Four also instructed the committee to commence preparations for minority protection agreements with Greece and Romania, as these countries "will receive large territorial increases."[9] The committee was also instructed to draft minority protection clauses for the Austrian, Hungarian, and Bulgarian peace treaties then under preparation. On May 13, the committee proposed to the Council of Four the insertion into the Austrian, Hungarian, and Bulgarian peace treaties of articles stating that Czechoslovakia, Yugoslavia, Romania, and Greece would conclude minority protection agreements with the Principal Powers. Its members had in mind clauses similar to those already inserted in the draft of the German peace treaty relating to Poland.[10] On May 22 the committee received the Council of Four's approval in this matter as well.[11]

The Drafting of Poland's
Minority Protection Treaty

Until the middle of May, the Commission on New States and Minorities concentrated its attention on compiling the text of the Polish treaty. The committee was instructed to include in the minority protection agreement paragraphs recognizing the new

Polish state and guaranteeing its sovereignty, as well as listing all its obligations necessary in the field of international trade and transportation.

On May 17 the Council of Four discussed and approved the work submitted by the committee.[12] The committee presented the Council of Four with alternatives on two issues; Headlam-Morley represented the committee at the meeting. One of the issues was whether or not problems specific to the individual minorities should be addressed at all. The committee suggested that in general such problems should not be dealt with, but that some requests applying to Jewish communities should be granted (for example, autonomous control of schools where instruction was in Yiddish, and regulations facilitating observance of the Sabbath). The Council of Four concurred in the committee's opinion and rejected the idea of listing the various nationalities and their specific interests, arguing that such a list would need to be complete and with Poland's eastern frontiers not yet drawn it was impossible to predict the precise ethnic composition of Poland's eventual minority population. Defending the decision to include passages dealing specifically with Jewish minorities, the Council of Four on the one hand pointed out that these demands were, indeed, specific (for example, in the matter of the Sabbath) and on the other hand referred to Poland's long history of anti-Semitism, which seemed to justify extra protection for this particular minority.

The other issue left to the decision of the Council of Four was whether or not to include in the agreement a passage permitting the minorities to approach the League of Nations directly with their grievances. The Council of Four decided against including such a passage in the agreement, arguing that, as in the case of autonomy, this right too would promote the organization of the minorities into *political* bodies, thus weakening the national character (the "political nation") of the new Polish state contrary to the demands, acknowledged by the victorious powers, of the Polish ruling élite. In fact, as it turned out, and as we shall see, the minorities were able to hand petitions directly to the League of Nations Secretariat, even though they were not formally entitled to do so.

The preparations for the minority protection treaty with

Poland ended with the May 17 session of the Council of Four. The committee was ordered to draw up the final text and to inform the Polish delegation to the Peace Conference about its content.

The draft treaty—which, apart from minor changes, was identical to the treaty later concluded between Poland and the five Principal Powers—can be divided thematically into four parts:[13]

1. *The recognition by the Powers of an independent Polish state.* The independence of the Polish nation, previously unlawfully suspended, was now restored with the help of the armies of the "Allied and Associated Powers." In addition, the rubric declared that the Polish state, which was exercising *de facto* sovereignty in areas populated largely by Poles, had already been recognized by the "Allied and Associated Powers" as a sovereign and independent state. This recognition was confirmed by the United States, Great Britain, France, Italy, and Japan in this treaty.

2. *The protection of minorities and international guarantees.* (This was dealt with in the twelve articles of Chapter 1 of the treaty.) A detailed account of the twelve articles seems justifiable on the grounds that the minority protection agreements concluded with the other states, as well as the minority protection clauses inserted in the peace treaties, were all modeled on the Polish minority protection treaty. These articles also serve to illustrate the principles of international minority protection devised after World War I.

In Article 1 Poland accepted the obligation to regard the following articles (Articles 2 to 8 inclusive) as "basic law." This meant that any laws, decrees, statutes, or official measures not in accordance with them would be considered null and void.

Article 2 stated that Poland undertook to assure full protection of life and liberty for its inhabitants "without distinction of birth, nationality, language, race, or religion."

Articles 3, 4, 5 and 6 specified the obligations of the state with regard to minorities. These amounted to a very important provision: they meant that no new state was free to make arbitrary decisions on the granting or denying of citizenship to members of minorities on its territory. These articles guaranteed people the right to continue living in their home area, and obligated the states to grant equal citizenship to all minorities resident within their new borders. At the same time, persons who had achieved minority status due to boundary changes were given the option of remaining at their place of residence and adopting new citizenship, or of retaining their former citizenship and leaving. This option, however, was only open for minority *persons;* the Polish state was not given the power to make the decision for them.

Article 7 ensured for the minority member equality before the law, together with equal civil and political rights. It stated that religious or denominational differences should play no part in filling state posts, jobs, and offices or in occupational opportunities.

The next paragraph of the same article was very important; it guaranteed the freedom of language use for all citizens. It reads:

> No restriction shall be imposed on the free use by any Polish national of any language in private intercourse, in commerce, in religion, in the press or in publications of any kind, or at public meetings.

The same article stated that citizens speaking a tongue different from the official language were free to use their mother-tongue, in speech and in writing, in the courts, and had to be given a guarantee that the state would give them due assistance in the exercise of this right.

Article 8, the last of the articles regarded as basic law, is again of sufficient importance to be quoted in full:

> Polish nationals who belong to racial, religious, or linguistic minorities shall enjoy the same treatment and security in law and in fact as other Polish nationals. In particular, they shall have an equal right to establish, manage, and control at their own expense charitable, religious, and social institutions, schools and other educational establishments with the right to use their own language and to exercise their religion freely therein.

Though not regarded as basic law, Article 9 supplemented Article 8. It said that where nationals speaking a non-Polish language lived "in considerable proportions," the government would help their children to receive elementary schooling in their own tongue. (This, however, could not invalidate the obligatory character of the teaching of the Polish language.) Moreover, a proportionate part of the budgetary appropriations for educational, religious, and charitable purposes had to be allocated to the racial, religious, and linguistic minorities.

Articles 10 and 11 contained further minority protection passages, applying to Jewish communities and complementing the above. The substance of Article 10 was that the organization and direction of Jewish schools and the distribution of the share allocated to them from public funds according to the provisions of Article 9 were to be administered by local school committees designated by the Jewish community, under the control of the state. Article 11 guaranteed the opportunity to observe the Sabbath.

Article 12, which closed the section on minority protection, contained the agreement by Poland that the above rights "constitute obligations of international concern and shall be placed under the guarantee of the League of Nations". Accordingly, Poland acknowledged that any member of the Council of the League of Nations had the right to call the attention of the Council to any breach of these obligations or to the threat of such a breach, and that in such cases the Council could take "proper and effective" action. Poland also agreed that any difference arising between it and any member of the Council of the League had to be regarded as a dispute of international character, which, according to the Covenant of the League of Nations, could, at the request of any Council member, be submitted to the judgment of the Permanent Court of International Justice. The decision of this world court was final, and was of the same force and effect as an award under Article 13 of the League of Nations Covenant.

3. *The rights of the Allied Powers.* Since the new Polish state was not bound by the international conventions, diplomatic or economic, signed by its former rulers, Articles 12 to 21 in the second part of the treaty covered some of the areas where such agreements were necessary. Article 13, for example, formed the basis for bilateral diplomatic and consular representation. Article 18 regulated navigation rights on the river Vistula international waterway. In Article 19, Poland agreed to the obligations con-

tained in the international telegraph conventions of 1875, 1908, and 1912 and those laid down in the international railway conventions of 1890 and 1907. In Article 21, Poland, as a former part of the Russian Empire, admitted liability, at least in principle, for a proportionate part of Russia's debts, the precise amount of which was to be fixed at later negotiations. Poland also agreed that if these negotiations broke down, the matter would be referred to the League of Nations for arbitration.

4. *The concluding part of the agreement.* In this final passage the method of ratification and the date of promulgation were fixed: the agreement was to take effect simultaneously with the German peace treaty.

The Plenary Session of May 31 and the Clash Between Brătianu and Wilson

In the second half of May, the work of the Peace Conference in the area of minority protection accelerated and became more complex. After the draft of the German peace treaty had been given to the delegates of the German government, the treaty with Austria was compiled; the intention was to hand it to the Austrian government by the end of May, keeping it separate from the Hungarian treaty, work on which was proceeding concurrently. Since the draft of the minority protection agreement to be concluded with Poland had been presented for preliminary study to the Polish delegation and to the Polish government, the minority committee then worked on the texts of the minority protection agreements to be signed with Czechoslovakia, Romania, the Serb-Croat-Slovene state, and Greece.

The peacemakers wished to arrange for the simultaneous signing of the German treaty and the agreement in which the five Principal Powers guaranteed Poland its sovereignty and prescribed its obligations in the field of minority protection. It was also their plan to have the work on the Austrian peace treaty run parallel to the work on the minority protection agreements with Czechoslovakia, Romania, and the Kingdom of Serbs, Croats and Slovenes, as Yugoslavia was then called.[14]

The minority protection accord with Greece was to be signed

at the same time as the Bulgarian and Turkish peace treaties. Through this planned linkage, the states signatory to the peace treaties received an additional signal that their co-nationals now living as minorities in the new or enlarged states would be guaranteed minority rights.

It was mentioned that Articles 86 and 93 of the peace treaty with Germany referred to the agreement by Czechoslovakia and Poland to conclude accords on the protection of their minorities and stated that the said accords would be guaranteed by the League of Nations. Similar clauses were now inserted into the draft of the Austrian peace treaty with regard to Czechoslovakia, Romania, and the Kingdom of Serbs, Croats, and Slovenes.[15]

Thus, as early as the second half of May, the Polish, Czechoslovak, Romanian, Yugoslav, and Greek governments were acquainted with the minority protection obligations the Principal Powers expected them to undertake. They rejected them, claiming that the provisions would constitute a violation of their sovereignty. They did not question the need for minority protection, but considered it a domestic matter, not a matter for international obligation. Only Czechoslovakia actually began to work out its own minority protection laws.

The sharpest protest was lodged by the Romanian government, led by Ion I. C. Brătianu.[16] At that time, Bucharest's dissatisfaction with the actions of the Council was becoming evident on other issues, too. In an interview given to the Paris's *Le Journal* on May 16, Brătianu heaped reproaches on the Council of Four: "it seems ... that the Big Four do not have a clear conception, since neither financially nor geographically will the treaty of peace bring us our due rewards." He continued: "Still, it was Romania which saved Saloniki, relieved Verdun, and stopped Bolshevism. [...] Without our armies Moscow and Budapest would have joined hands and reached Vienna."[17]

On May 23, the minorities committee—having decided at its May 21 session in favor of the need for a minority protection agreement to be concluded with Romania—sent a letter to Brătianu.[18] In this the committee indicated that it was familiar with the Transylvanian government's declaration (probably a reference to the resolution adopted by the assembly held at Gyulafehérvár) which guaranteed "full autonomy as regards local administration, education, and religion" to the Hungarian, Saxon, Szekler, and other minorities, and that while the members of the committee assumed that the Romanian government concurred with this policy, they would still have liked to receive first-hand information concerning the Romanian government's intentions with regard to the minorities.[19] As Brătianu wrote to the minorities committee on May 27, the Royal Government of Romania had

> decided to assure throughout the new Kingdom the rights and liberties of minorities by a generous decentralization of the administration so as to guarantee to alien populations free development in their language, education and worship. But Romania will agree to such obligations only if every member of the League of Nations undertakes similar obligations with regard to its own territory.[20]

On the next day, the Council of Four rejected the Romanian protest and approved the inclusion in the drafts of the Austrian and Hungarian peace treaties of passages holding Romania to international minority protection obligations similar to those formulated in Articles 86 and 93 of the peace treaty with Germany.[21]

May 29 and 31, the Peace Conference held a plenary meeting to approve the text of the Austrian peace treaty before handing it to the representatives of the Austrian government. The draft contained the articles which referred to the readiness of the Czechoslovak, Romanian, and Yugoslav governments to conclude agreements in which they accepted minority protection obligations. At the May 31 session, a heated discussion arose.[22] The top-level representatives of the new or enlarged states on which the obligation of minority protection was to be imposed requested the deletion of the articles in question, although—with the exception of Brătianu—they eventually accepted the decision of the Peace Conference. Brătianu, who repeatedly addressed the meeting, even went as far as to state that, should the offending passages be included in the peace treaty with Austria, his government would not sign it.[23]

The position of the Principal Powers was most comprehensively expounded by Wilson. Above all, he explained to the protesters, it was for the sake of their countries that the Principal Powers insisted on minority protection and the international guaranteeing of it; this was the only way to turn the minorities into real citizens and to prevent them from becoming potential enemies of the state, and the only way to ensure peace. Wilson also pointed out that it was the efforts and military victories of the Principal Powers that had made possible the formation of new states and the expansion of others already in existence; for this reason, they, the Principal Powers, had the right to impose certain requirements, the more so since these would promote the common objective of ensuring world peace.

Wilson sharply rejected Brătianu's arguments that the Principal Powers, which insisted on minority protection for the sake of lasting peace, would thereby violate Romania's sovereignty:

> I beg [Mr. Brătianu] to observe that he is overlooking the fact that he is asking the sanction of the allied and associated powers for great additions of territory which come to Roumania by the common victory of arms, and that, therefore, we are entitled to say: "If we agree to these additions of territory, we have the right to insist upon certain guarantees of peace."*

Directly after the plenary meeting of the Peace Conference, the Council of Four held a meeting and decided that even after the debate that developed at the meeting it would not change the draft of the Austrian peace treaty.[24] On June 2, the document was presented to the Austrian delegation for preliminary study.

---

* The full text of Wilson's speech can be found in Appendix 1.

Signing the Polish Treaty—Clemenceau's
Accompanying Letter

The firm decision of the Principal Powers to conclude the minority protection agreements became apparent not only at the May 31 discussions, but also from the fact that the Council of Four refused to make substantial changes in the text of the finished minority protection accord which had already been presented to Poland.

On June 15, a lengthy memorandum concerning Poland's minority protection treaty arrived from Ignacy Paderewski, the Polish prime minister. First of all, Paderewski reiterated the objections of the new and the enlarged states which centered on the alleged violations of sovereignty: "The Polish state, sovereign in principle, would thus be permanently placed under the control of the Powers." His argument against the insertion of the articles dealing specifically with the Jewish minority was interesting. According to Paderewski, these articles would make assimilation more difficult, and for this reason a significant percentage of Poland's Jews opposed them:

The stipulations proposed with regard to the rights of the Jewish population will call forth a deep resentment towards that part of the Jewish population which, whilst attached to its religion, considers itself to be of Polish nationality and is anxious to avoid a conflict with Poles over national and linguistic rights.

In addition, Paderewski pointed to the strange anomaly that, while Poland would be bound to protect its German minority, no obligations would be placed on Germany with regard to its own Polish minority, as would normally have been demanded in the interests of reciprocity.[25]

On June 17, the Council of Four discussed Paderewski's memorandum and found it unacceptable. On one point, however, Wilson was sympathetic to the Polish prime minister's case: this concerned the lack of reciprocity between Poland and Germany in obligations to their respective minorities. The whole issue was referred to the minorities commission for study and recommendations.[26] On June 21, the Council of Four, having received the committee's report, returned to the problem.[27] In the end, the Polish proposal that Germany also be bound to the protection of minorities—a proposal to which Wilson had shown sympathy a few days earlier—was rejected; the committee argued that the size and situation of the minorities in the two countries were substantially different. At the same time, a resolution was adopted which said that, should a sizeable Polish minority be attached to Germany after the forthcoming plebiscite in Upper Silesia, the protection of the Polish population of Silesia would have to be put back on the agenda.

On June 23, the Council of Four discussed Paderewski's memorandum for the last time. At the meeting, Lloyd George agreed in principle with the Polish prime minister that the minority protection treaties should not hinder assimilation. He went on to argue—in sharp contrast with the views of the Polish prime minister—that Articles 10 and 11 would promote assimilation rather than hinder it. "Every effort ought to be made," he said, "to help the Jews of Poland to merge into the Polish nationality, just as the Jews in Great Britain or France became merged in British or French nationality."[28]

The acceptance of some Polish remarks resulted in minor modifications to the wording of the text. The treaty to be concluded with Poland was now given its final form and was approved. Together with an accompanying letter signed by Clemenceau, it was handed to the Polish government on June 24. Simultaneously it was made known that the signing of the treaty was scheduled for June 28, the same date that the signature of the German peace treaty was due. The accompanying letter signed by Clemenceau is an important document revealing the goals of minority protection and the thinking which lay behind them. Since it constituted the first official statement by the Supreme Council on the subject, it deserves detailed study.*

The introduction to the accompanying letter made clear the interconnectedness between the following:

a) the Principal Powers' recognition of Poland as an independent state;

---

* For the full text, see Appendix 2.

b) the signing of the German peace treaty approving the transfer to Poland of certain areas which formerly belonged to Germany;

c) Poland's acceptance of the treaty guaranteeing the protection of minorities.

The decision by the Principal Powers that the peace treaty with Germany and the agreement with Poland on the protection of minorities would be signed simultaneously on June 28 further emphasized this interconnectedness. The fact that Paderewski, immediately after dispatching his June 15 memorandum summarizing his objections, signaled that Poland was nevertheless willing to sign the minority protection treaty indicated that he, too, was aware of it.

The accompanying letter briefly elucidated the treaty and the thinking which lay behind it. Explaining that it was customary in European international law that the Great Powers linked the recognition of a new state with international conventions concerning certain governmental principles of the new state, this communication contained quotations from the speeches made at the June 28 session of the Congress of Berlin by Salisbury, Waddington, Bismarck, Launay, and Andrássy. Moreover, the Polish government was assured that the treaty served the interests not only of Poland's stability, but also of peace in the region. Moreover, Warsaw was told that such treaties were to be concluded with all the new or enlarged states, and that the aims of the Principal Powers and Poland were identical.

Although the treaty was to be signed by the five Principal Powers, this would give them no right to interfere in Poland's internal affairs: the League of Nations was to be entrusted with the task of enforcing the guarantees.

There were a number of linguistically distinct minority groups living in Poland. It seemed that they would reconcile themselves to their new circumstances more easily if they could be sure of some protection and adequate guarantees against all forms of unfair treatment and oppression.

On June 27, one day before signature, the Council of Four discussed the text of the treaty for the last time in the presence of Paderewski, since in a letter dated June 26 the Polish prime minister had asked for two last-minute modifications.[29] One concerned the above-mentioned principle of reciprocity, which would have demanded that Germany also be obliged by international guarantee to afford protection to the Polish minority living within its borders. The Supreme Council agreed to this in principle, although the members thought that it was already too late in the day to modify the German peace treaty. They suggested that Paderewski directly approach either the German government or the League of Nations in the matter. The other modification concerned the finer points of governmental supervision of the Yiddish schools, which, in the view of the Council of Four, fell outside the scope of the minority protection treaty.

On June 28, during a plenary session of the Peace Conference held in the Hall of Mirrors in the Palace of Versailles, Germany signed its peace treaty with the Allied and Associated Powers. Also, a treaty covering the military occupation of the Ruhr area was signed by the United States, Belgium, Britain, and France on the one side, and by Germany on the other. Finally, the five Principal Powers and Poland signed the treaty which, simultaneously, recognized the new Polish state and protected its minorities under international law.[30] The same day the Covenant of the League of Nations was also signed.

Czechoslovakia's Minority Protection Treaty

After signing the German peace treaty and the guarantee of the minority protection agreement with Poland, the final formulation took place of the minority protection treaties to be concluded with Czechoslovakia, Yugoslavia, and Romania. The Principal Powers wished to have these signed simultaneously with the next —the Austrian—peace treaty; the preparatory work with the Czechoslovak government progressed smoothly.

The Czechoslovak delegation was led by Foreign Minister Eduard Beneš, who co-operated actively with the Commission on New States and Minorities and with the Council of Four concerning the minority protection agreement to be concluded with Czechoslovakia. This co-operation was particularly useful in working out the treaty on autonomy for Sub-Carpathian Ruthenia, in the far east of the country.[31]

At the inception of the minority protection work, the Council of Four—as already mentioned—did not insist on the granting of autonomy to the minorities. Of course, its stand did not exclude this option; the leading Allied powers merely took the view that autonomy could not be considered a fundamental minority right which needed to be guaranteed. Consequently, in its initial form the draft agreement with Czechoslovakia was simply a restatement of the general principles of the Polish treaty. Beneš himself pointed out at the discussions of the committee that his government favored those movements and forces that tended towards federative development in Czechoslovakia, adding, however, that the time was not yet right for the implementing of decentralization.

Nevertheless, Beneš said that he would support the inclusion in the treaty of the idea of territorial autonomy for Sub-Carpathian Ruthenia. Thus, four new articles (Articles 10 to 13) were added to the minority protection treaty with Czechoslovakia, according to which the Ruthenian area within Czechoslovakia was to be granted "the fullest degree of self-government compatible with the unity of the Czecho-Slovak state." The politically autonomous territory would have its own local assembly, vested with legislative powers in linguistic, educational, religious, and local government matters.[32]

Thus, nothing obstructed the signature of the guarantee and minority protection agreement with regard to Czechoslovakia when, simultaneously, the Austrian peace treaty was concluded.

The Minority Protection Passage in the Austrian Peace Treaty

Article 51 of the Austrian peace treaty referred to the obligation of the Serb-Croat-Slovene state to conclude a minority protection agreement with the Principal Powers. Similar in content were Article 57 with regard to Czechoslovakia and Article 60 with regard to Romania. Essentially, these articles were drawn up along the same lines as described in connection with the German treaty.

Articles 62 to 69 inclusive in Chapter V, which was entitled "Protection of Minorities," contained the relevant regulations. Article 62 (which was similar in wording to Article 1 of the Polish treaty) established that the provisions in the Chapter had the force of basic law. Article 63 was identical to Article 2 of the Polish treaty. Articles 64 and 65 dealt with the citizenship or residence options of minorities. Article 66 was identical to Article 7, Article 67 to Article 8, and Article 68 to Article 9 of the Polish treaty; Article 69 corresponded to Article 12.

All the peace treaties with Germany's former allies—including the one with Austria—differed from the German treaty in one important respect: they contained minority protection clauses basically similar from the point of view of principles to those included in the minority protection agreement with Poland. With regard to the Austrian and Hungarian peace treaties, the Council of Four made its decision at its May 28 meeting.[33]

Minority protection chapters with texts similar to the relevant passage of the Austrian peace treaty were included in each peace treaty— except for the one with Germany. Although the significantly diminished loser states did not include minorities in the same numbers and degree as the new and enlarged states, they did nevertheless contain minorities; because of the national antagonisms exacerbated by the hostilities, the extension of internationally guaranteed minority protection to these was also justified. The new Bulgaria had a minority population of 16 percent, or about 875,000 persons. Hungary's minority nationalities now amounted to 10 percent of the total population and numbered 830,000. Few members of ethnic minorities were left in Austria: only 215,000 people, or 3.3 percent of the total number of inhabitants. European Turkey contained a minority population of 210,000, about 20 percent of those living there.[34]

Compared to the 22.5-million minority population of the "winner states" (Poland, Czechoslovakia, Yugoslavia, Romania, and Greece), the minority population of the "loser states" (a total of only 2.2 million) was small. Even so, the protection of these 2.2 million people was warranted.

It is, however, somewhat surprising that Germany, which, according to its 1925 census, had a minority population of 1.2 million, was not required to protect the non-German elements of its population. These 1.2 million people lived largely in areas the status of which had been decided by plebiscite. When the text of the German peace treaty was formulated and when the treaty was signed, the number of national minority members likely to elect to live in Germany was insignificant indeed.[35] However, as a result of the plebiscites, Germany ultimately acquired a rather large Polish minority (or, to be more exact, a bilingual population speaking German and Polish), chiefly in Silesia. A German-Polish treaty, subsequently guaranteed by the League of Nations, provided for the protection of this group. In this way international minority protection was extended to the vast majority of national minority members living in Germany.

On June 2, the draft proposal of the Austrian peace treaty was handed over by Clemenceau to the Austrian delegation led by Chancellor Renner. Requesting certain changes, the Austrian delegation delivered a number of notes, and not without success. The delegation's claim to the Burgenland was accepted, as well as its appeal that plebiscites be held to decide the fate of Klagenfurt and that of the surrounding Klagenfurt Basin. The final text of the Austrian treaty was handed to the delegation on September 2, and on September 10 the documents were signed.

Despite the fact that the treaties to be concluded with Yugoslavia and Romania were also ready for signature, only the minority protection agreement between Czechoslovakia and the Principal Powers was actually signed: the Pašić and the Brătianu governments avoided signing the relevant documents. Furthermore, since the Austrian peace treaty contained references to the willingness of the "Serb, Croat, and Slovene State" and the Kingdom of Romania to conclude minority protection agreements with the Principal Powers, Pašić and Brătianu refused for the time being to sign this instrument as well.

The Commission on New States and Minorities and the Supreme Council of the Conference—after the Council of Four had concluded its work with the signature of the German treaty, it came to be called the Council of Heads of Delegations—had to conduct difficult negotiations with the Yugoslav and Romanian governments before they were willing to sign.

The Yugoslav Minority Protection Treaty

The difficulty with the minority protection treaty to be concluded with the Serb-Croat-Slovene state was caused not only by the need to overcome the resistance of the Pašić government, but also by the disagreement existing among the Principal Powers about the formulation of its contents.

At first, Pašić expressed the view that the Yugoslav state was not new but, rather, the same as the old Kingdom of Serbia; consequently, unlike Poland and Czechoslovakia, it was not a new state formation, and there was therefore no historical basis for obligatory minority protection. The Principal Powers were united in their rejection of this argument; they pointed out that Serbia's territorial acquisitions as a result of the Balkan Wars of 1912 and 1913 had not yet been approved. As a result, in exchange for recognition of the Yugoslav state, the Principal Powers insisted on the protection of minorities not only in areas added as a result of the World War, but also throughout the entire territory of the state. It was on the basis of this position that in July 1919 the Commission on New States and Minorities began drawing up the treaty to be concluded with Yugoslavia. This was after the Polish treaty had been signed and after the text of the Czechoslovak treaty had been agreed upon with the Prague government, and was merely waiting to be signed.

There was no argument in the committee with respect to the general articles—which were also included in the texts of the agreements with Poland and Czechoslovakia—but heated disputes developed over the issue of whether autonomy similar to that granted to Czechoslovakian Sub-Carpathian Ruthenia was justified for Yugoslavia's Albanians and Macedonians. The debate was further complicated by the concurrent Serb-Italian conflict, very bitter at the time, which manifested itself in demands from the Italian delegate for stringent minority protection obligations: at the July 10 and 15 sessions he argued that, analogously to the territorial autonomy of the Ruthene population in the draft Czechoslovak treaty, autonomy for Serbia's Albanian and Macedonian populations was also warranted. The French delegate opposed autonomy in both cases, but the British delegate supported autonomy for Macedonia, although less definitively than the Italian proposal. Finally, the committee decided to inform the Yugoslav government concerning the alternatives considered and to request its own views on minority policy.

Nikola Pašić, Yugoslavia's prime minister and also the head of the Yugoslav delegation to the Peace Conference, replied in writing to the committee on August 1. He attempted to justify the rejection of minority protection obligations for Yugoslavia using a new set of arguments:

> The Serb-Croat-Slovene State, composed of a single people with three names, three religions and two alphabets, by its very nature is called upon to practise the broadest tolerance... Consequently, the question concerning the protection of minorities in this State cannot have practical scope.

With specific reference to the Macedonian question, Pašić's argument was that a "Macedon ethnic minority" did not exist at all: the Slavs living there had always been considered Serbs. Moreover, their civic and political equality was already ensured and did not require any additional protection. As to the religious worship and culture of Moslems, the Serbian-Turkish Treaty of March 14, 1914 was sufficient guarantee, and the vast majority of the Moslems in the area were of Serbian nationality anyway. In this way Pašić tried to depict multinational Yugoslavia as a "national" state; moreover, reiterating his position of May 31, he rejected international protection for minorities on the grounds that it would violate the sovereignty of the Yugoslav state.[36]

It was after such preliminaries that the matter came before the Supreme Council on September 1. By then completion of the final text, and approval of the text by the Supreme Council, had become urgent, since the Austrian peace treaty was due to be signed on September 10. Pašić signaled—and the Supreme Council took note of this at its August 31 session—that he would not sign the Austrian treaty without knowing the precise content of the minority protection agreement setting out Yugoslavia's obligations (these were mentioned in Article 59 of the Austrian treaty).[37]

By this time Lloyd George and Wilson were no longer participating in the work of the Supreme Council; Clemenceau was its most prestigious member. Frank L. Polk represented the United States, Balfour the British government, while Italy and Japan were represented by Tommaso Tittoni and K. Matsui respectively. The Englishman James Headlam-Morley was appointed to present the views of the Commission on New States and Minorities on the Yugoslav situation; Clemenceau's influence at the meeting was overwhelming.

From the outset, the French were opposed to the inclusion of any autonomy in the Yugoslav minority protection treaty, and the Supreme Council now discarded the passage referring to Macedonian autonomy. But since the Supreme Council, unlike Pašić, regarded the Macedonians as a "minority" rather than as Serbs, it still insisted that full minority protection be extended to them. Accordingly, the final draft—final for the time being, that is—contained the same general minority rights that had been laid down in the Polish treaty. Only Article 10, which safeguarded specific Moslem interests and contained, among other things, the appointment of Reis-ül-Ülema, could be considered in any way different.[38]

Even in this form, Pašić refused to accept the completed draft handed to him in accordance with the Supreme Council's decision. In a letter dated September 4 but not presented to the Supreme Council until September 8 (two days before the document was due to be signed) the Yugoslav prime minister expressed the objection that the draft concerned itself with areas acquired by Serbia as a result of the two Balkan wars—areas with which the World War had nothing to do. He also objected to the fact that the text of the treaty referred to the "State of Serbs, Croats and Slovenes," and not to the "Serb-Croat-Slovene State," the correct name expressing the unity of the nation.[39]

The treaty should have been signed on September 10, concurrently with the Austrian peace treaty. Although it had now softened its earlier total opposition, the Pašić government still refused, for the time being, to sign both the minority protection treaty and the Austrian peace treaty.

However, the Supreme Council remained determined to extract from the Southern Slav Kingdom the protection of minorities in return for recognizing its sovereign power over the newly-acquired lands. This determination was evident in its resolution of October 29, precluding the Serb-Croat-Slovene delegation from signing the Bulgarian peace treaty until it had signed the Austrian peace treaty and the minority protection agreement.[40] Since Greece alone was mentioned in the Bulgarian peace treaty in connection with minority protection obligations (Article 46),[41] under normal circumstances it would have been possible for Yugoslavia and Romania to sign this treaty, even if they refused to sign the minority protection agreement. The Bulgarian peace treaty contained no minority obligations with regard to Bulgaria's other two neighbors, because the border between Bulgaria and Romania remained entirely unchanged and because the border changes between Bulgaria and Serbia affected the minority populations only slightly.

The Supreme Council was quite determined to demand internationally-guaranteed minority protection from Yugoslavia, but at the same time it did not want disputes with the Pašić government. Accordingly, the Supreme Council instructed the committee, then working on the minority protection agreement, to seek further compromise. After additional talks lasting for almost two more months, a suitable text was formulated. Apart from some formal changes (the wording and spelling of the state name as advocated by Pašić was the most important of these), the basic compromise consisted of the Supreme Council's ensuring the extension of minority protection throughout the entire territory of the state, while Pašić succeeded in restricting the applicability of Article 9 to only the areas acquired after January 1, 1913—areas which did not contain Albanians and Macedonians. The article, a verbatim copy of Article 9 of the Polish treaty, provided that wherever a significant proportion of the inhabitants belonged to a minority, the government had to ensure elementary schooling for the children in their mother-tongue. Furthermore, the state and local authorities had to allocate from their budgets proportionate subsidies to the minorities for educational and religious purposes.

Obviously, the applicability of Article 9 made it harder for the children of the Albanian and Macedonian minorities to receive schooling in their mother-tongues and to foster their own national cultures. But at the same time, Article 8 did apply to them: they were free to establish, at their own expense, schools and cultural institutions operating in their mother-tongues. (It should be noted that a similar compromise was effected in the provisions of the Polish peace treaty. In the original draft, Article 9 of this treaty also had general validity, but because the Polish government objected to the absence of similar minority protection for Poles in Germany, it was modified in order to limit its applicability to the German minority only in the territories formerly belonging to Germany but now transferred to Poland.)

In accordance with these compromises, the text of the minority treaty was modified, but its original date of September 10 was not changed. (This explains why historiography generally mentions the treaty as though it had been concluded or signed on September 10.) On December 5, the Yugoslav delegation in Paris issued a declaration bearing the signatures of Pašić, Ante Trumbić, and Ivan Zolger. In this these statesmen agreed to accept without reservation the peace treaty concluded with Austria, as well as the minority protection agreement between the Principal Powers and the Serb-Croat-Slovene Kingdom.[42]

The Romanian Minority Protection Treaty

For the Supreme Council, which insisted on the conclusion of minority protection treaties, the hardest nut to crack was without doubt the Romanian prime minister, Ion I. C. Brătianu. According to the original plans of the Supreme Council, as mentioned earlier, the Czechoslovakian, Yugoslavian, and Romanian minority protection treaties were to have been signed at the same time as the Austrian peace treaty, just as the German peace treaty was signed at the same time as the Polish minority protection treaty.

Accordingly, as the Commission on New States and Minorities proceeded with its work on the text of the Yugoslav treaty, the text of the Romanian treaty proceeded more or less in parallel.

The minorities committee had its first comprehensive talks with regard to the *contents* of the minority protection treaty to be concluded with Romania on June 7. The committee agreed that the general articles should correspond to the already completed Polish and Czechoslovakian drafts. A debate developed as to whether two special passages from the Polish treaty draft which referred to the Jews should be included. For the time being, the question was left open. The British member of the committee proposed additional assurances for the historically-established local autonomy enjoyed by Transylvania's Szeklers and Saxons. This proposal, which was supported by the Italian member, temporarily remained open.[43] Three days later, however, the British pressed for an answer on this issue and a positive decision was made.

By July 16, the first full draft of the treaty was ready; it was discussed at the committee session of the same day and sent to the Supreme Council, together with a lengthy report by way of justification.[44]

In its report in support of the draft, the committee adopted its position over the earlier Romanian objection that Romania—unlike Czechoslovakia and Yugoslavia—was in essence a homogeneous national state where similar minority problems were out of the question. The committee stated:

> The greater Roumania of the future will not be a homogeneous state with respect to race, language, or religion, though it is to be hoped that all the varied elements of the nation will feel a common loyalty to the Roumanian government: indeed it is to this end that the treaty stipulations are devised. There will be large populations speaking Magyar, German, Russian, Bulgarian, Serbian, and other tongues, who will pass under Roumanian sovereignty; there will be churches, schools and courts, in which other languages than the Roumanian have been employed, in the regions now united with the Kingdom of Roumania.

Accordingly, the committee was of the opinion that a minority protection treaty was also absolutely justified in the case of Romania.

The draft was in complete agreement with the general articles of the Polish, Czechoslovak, and Yugoslav minority protection treaties and the minority protection chapters of the Austrian peace treaty. It had, however, two additional parts—one of which applied to Jews and the other which dealt with the Szeklers and Saxons.

The committee considered the status of the Jews of Romania to be similar to that of the Jews in Poland, in other words unlike the status enjoyed by the emancipated and assimilated Jewry of Western and Central Europe: "They form a minority, not only religious but also national." Moreover, the committee also took into account the fact that "in the region recently ceded to Roumania the percentage of Jewish population is very high." This applied to the Bukovina region and also to Bessarabia. (In the Introduction it was pointed out that the Jews of Transylvania regarded themselves as Hungarians.) In the case of Bessarabia the final and formal decision concerning sovereignty had not yet been made by the Principal Powers; the territory was under *de facto* Romanian control and the Principal Powers had already accepted Romania's demand for it. Therefore, the committee deemed it necessary to include passages corresponding to Articles 10 and 11 of the Polish treaty. When discussing the Polish treaty, we saw that Wilson thought the inclusion of the special passages necessary in order to combat the strong anti-Semitic sentiment prevalent in that country. There were similar considerations in Romania's case also: the delaying tactics employed with regard to the emancipation of Romanian Jewry were clear to everyone. In practice, Romania had not fulfilled its obligations (undertaken in the Treaty of Berlin, 1878, in which the Great Powers had recognized the newly-sovereign state of Romania) to guarantee the equality of civil liberties for all religious denominations. In 1902, the U.S. government called the attention of the Royal Romanian Government to this deficiency in an official document (the Hay Memorandum). After the Second Balkan War, in the summer of 1913, another such protest was made by the United States government, this time during Wilson's presidency. Neither of these interventions yielded any result: they were rejected outright.[45]

The article referring to Saxons and Szeklers—which was included without change in the final text—reads: "Roumania agrees to accord to the communities of the Saxons and Szeklers in Transylvania local autonomy in regard to scholastic and religious matters, under the control of the Roumanian State."

The committee's justification of the wording of the article is worthy of note:

The presence of the Saxon and Szekler enclaves in Transylvania makes it appear desirable that a small measure of cultural autonomy should be given to them if their community traditions and strong local sentiment are to be harmonized with the broader national patriotism, instead of coming into conflict with it.

At this point we should pay attention to the fact that at a later stage of the talks, when the Romanian government was showing willingness to sign a minority protection agreement and wished only to make modifications in the text, it did not object to the special articles referring to the Saxons and Szeklers.

The complete text of the draft, prepared by the committee by June 16, was discussed and approved by the Supreme Council on August 6. On August 7 and 9, the committee put the finishing touches to the draft,[46] and it was passed to the Romanian delegation by way of the Secretariat. However, no reply came from the Romanians. On August 29, the Secretariat requested—again without result—that the Romanian delegation acknowledge receipt of the draft and asked whether it had any comments to make.[47]

The conflict existing at the time between the Romanian delegation, or the Brătianu government, and the Supreme Council was not limited to the question of minority protection. While admittedly this problem constituted one of the main sources of conflict, it was the Brătianu government's foreign policy toward Hungary which lay at the root of it.

In the early days of August 1919, the Romanian army, then engaged in overthrowing the Hungarian Soviet Republic, enjoyed approval in Paris. However, shortly afterwards reports concerning the behavior of the Romanian troops (and the intentions of the Romanian government) arrived indicating that Bucharest, far from helping to stabilize the region, was in fact hindering consolidation.

The Supreme Council learned from the reports sent by the Entente Missions in Budapest that Brătianu, in order to legitimize the continuing Romanian occupation and to organize the transportation of Hungarian property to Romania as war reparations, was trying to force the new government, led by Gyula Peidl, to sign the appropriate armistice. On August 5, the Romanians delivered an ultimatum to this effect—to be answered within four hours—to the Peidl government.[48] The trade-union government resigned in the face of this pressure, but the Friedrich government which succeeded it was no more willing to sign such an armistice.

On August 6, the Supreme Council passed a resolution which was immediately forwarded to the Romanian authorities concerned. This stated that the Romanian commander-in-chief in Hungary had no right to conclude an armistice without authorization from the Allied and Associated Powers.[49]

It was also at this session that the Supreme Council decided to hand over to the Romanian delegation the text of the minority protection treaty to be concluded with Romania; this also shows that the two issues, which were causing increasingly strained relations between the Supreme Council and Romania, were closely interconnected.[50]

Although the firm stance taken by the Supreme Council prevented Romania from forcing an armistice on Hungary, this was enough neither to make Romania withdraw its army from Budapest and the eastern half of the country nor to put an end to the shipment to Romania of Hungarian assets—on which the other victorious powers demanding reparations also had a claim. In addition, Brătianu also wanted to reopen certain border disputes already settled by the Conference. Most notably, he demanded the redrawing of Romania's border with Hungary on the basis of the secret 1916 Treaty of Bucharest[51] and demanded territory in eastern Galicia in addition to the (already awarded) Bukovina. (Galicia and the Bukovina had formerly belonged to Austria.) Also, in the matter of the still-unresolved border disputes in Dobrudja and Bessarabia, Brătianu pressed for a quick decision in favor of Romania.

Therefore, the Brătianu government's confrontation with the Supreme Council was somewhat wide-ranging, and served to frustrate the Principal Powers' plans for the consolidation. Romania's conduct began to annoy even Clemenceau, the chief negotiator. At the September 2 meeting, it was Clemenceau himself who proposed the sending of an ultimatum to Romania.[52] The following day, Balfour was appointed to prepare the draft of the ultimatum.[53] Nicolae Misu, the head of the Romanian delegation in Paris, immediately wrote a letter to the chairman of the Supreme Council, and this was read to the members of the Council at the beginning of their next session. According to this letter, Romania was doing a great favor to the general cause.[54] Although this well-timed letter was not entirely ineffective, the Supreme Council approved the draft of the "ultimatum" (phrased rather mildly by Balfour) which specified the deadline for the withdrawal from Hungary, ordered the surrender of the evacuated assets, and called for Romania's loyalty to the Principal Powers.[55] The letter, addressed directly to the government, was taken to Bucharest by Sir George Clerk. The Supreme Council's firm stance against Romania was more than offset by its decision, taken the following day, in the matter of the Dobrudja: the Romanian-Bulgarian frontier, drawn in Romania's favor in 1913 following the Second Balkan War, was to remain.[56] Bulgaria, defeated in that conflict, had been forced to cede that strip of the Dobrudja which was inhabited by Bulgarians. Now, the 1913 frontier was confirmed.

Neither the delivery of the "ultimatum," nor the settling of the Dobrudja border to the satisfaction of Bucharest was able to alter the Romanian position with regard to the minority protection agreement, which was due to be signed on September 10, together with the Austrian peace treaty. The Romanian delegation—like the Yugoslav delegation—absented itself. Thus, only the Czechoslovak minority protection treaty was signed at the same time as the Austrian peace treaty.

Clerk arrived in Bucharest with the "ultimatum" on September 12. It was on the same day that Brătianu resigned as Romanian prime minister, although he now headed a "caretaker" government as such. Brătianu avoided all serious discussions by referring to the "caretaker" character of the administration. He surrendered his office to Arthur Văitoianu on September 29, the same day that Clerk left Bucharest.[57]

In the Supreme Council only the United States delegate took the ultimatum seriously; everybody else was seeking a compromise. However, the Văitoianu (i.e. Brătianu) leadership stuck to its maximum demands, and refused any compromise. Finally, the Supreme Council thought it necessary to send a "real" ultimatum. "My patience is utterly exhausted," said Clemenceau at the November 12 session of the Supreme Council. "The Romanians have always tried to prolong *pourparlers* indefinitely, and a stop must be put to this." Berthelot was entrusted with the task of wording the new ultimatum.[58]

The letter prepared by Berthelot and addressed to the Romanian government was discussed on November 13; the decision to send it, after certain modifications, was made on November 15. The ultimatum, this time intended to be serious, contained three demands: 1) Romania's withdrawal from Hungary, 2) the handing over of requisitioned property to the Inter-Allied Commission, and 3) Romania's signature of the Austrian peace treaty and the minority protection agreement.[59]

A "real" change of direction brought in a new government that was ready to accept a compromise with the Supreme Council. This was formed on December 5 by Alexandru Vaida-Voevod, and declared itself willing to meet the expectations of the Supreme Council, including the signing of the minority protection treaty. In the elections held in November, the new government, which had the joint support of the Romanian National Party of Transylvania and the union of old Romania's peasant parties, gained a majority.[60]

Although the Vaida-Voevod government was ready to sign the minority protection agreement, it insisted on certain modifications: these the Supreme Council accepted without debate, since no substantial alteration was involved. The new Romanian government accepted without comment the general articles, as well as the special clause dealing with the cultural autonomy of the Saxons and Szeklers. However, it did object to the other special clauses and provisions.

In particular, the Vaida-Voevod government objected to the part of the preamble which declared that with the signature of the minority treaty, which specified obligations towards the League of Nations, Romania's commitments to certain Great Powers, undertaken in the 1878 Treaty of Berlin, were to be null and void. Of course, Romania was not keen to endure these obligations, quite the contrary in fact: it wished to avoid all mention of them. Originally, this sentence was inserted in the preamble of the Yugoslav minority protection treaty at the express wish of Pašić. The committee drafting the Romanian treaty presumed (quite understandably, considering that the declaration actually released Romania from an existing obligation) that Romania would also insist on the inclusion of it.

Pašić had good reason to ask for the invalidation of the Treaty of Berlin. It was obvious, even without special provisions, that, by signing the new treaty with the Serb-Croat-Slovene government, the Great Powers would surrender their former right (laid down in the Berlin treaty) to intervene. The problem was that the signatories of the new treaty did not include all the powers which had signed the old one: Germany, Russia, and Austria-Hungary were not among them. Therefore, in line with international law, Germany could—in the absence of an annulment—subsequently submit demands on the basis of the 1878 treaty.

Interestingly, the subject had already been raised at the June 16 meeting of the Council of Four, when the proposal of the Commission on New States and Minorities was discussed concerning the possibility of inserting in the German peace treaty a passage rescinding Germany's right to supervise minority rights in the Balkan peninsula, as guaranteed in the 1878 treaty. In the end, the inclusion of such a passage was voted down. Perhaps Pašić also knew about this proposal; in any case, he requested the invalidation in writing of this particular passage of the Treaty of Berlin.

For the same reasons it is clear that the declaration would also have been advantageous, or even necessary, for Romania. However, Bucharest took the opposite view, although it never gave its reasons for doing so. The British diplomatic historian H.W.V. Temperley, the first person ever to compile a scholarly study of the Peace Conference, was rather baffled by the Romanian position. Nevertheless, his explanation was correct, albeit far from complete.

The attitude of the Roumanians on this point is not easy to understand. They seem to have regarded the whole system with such dislike that they repudiated any reference to it and they carried this attitude to such a degree that they would not accept even a formal discharge from their obligations; they preferred to act as if they did not exist.[61]

This interpretation, however, does not help explain the difference between the Yugoslavian and the Romanian positions, as the attitude described by Temperley fitted the Pašić government just as well. However, the relevant passage in the preamble was important to the Pašić government from another point of view, since it was Pašić himself who requested it. Pašić was repeatedly claiming that the Serb-Croat-Slovene state was not a new formation, but the extension of the Serb state with additional Serbian territories.

According to Pašić, the Serbs were one nation with three names. His view was that no fundamental change had taken place: no new state had been formed and the change was purely quantitative. The release of the Serb-Croat-Slovene Kingdom from obligations undertaken by the Kingdom of Serbia in 1878 seemed to support Pašić's theory of "continuity." Pašić was probably thinking of this argument when he asked for the inclusion of the above-mentioned passage. Obviously, Romania's politicians were not faced with the problem of having to prove the continuity of their state, as in Romania's case even the official name of the state (the Kingdom of Romania) remained unchanged.

The other modification, equally interesting, raised problems on the theoretical level. The new Romanian government opposed the inclusion of passages (corresponding to Articles 10 and 11 of the Polish treaty) specifically intended to protect the country's Jewish minority. The main argument advanced by the Romanian leadership was that it was equal rights, rather than some form of segregation, that the Jews of Romania were demanding, and that the general articles guaranteed the equality of rights to all minorities. With no contemporary surveys to rely on, it would be very difficult to determine the truth of this statement.

It is a fact that Berthelot, who was a member of the minorities committee and by virtue of this enjoyed access to the relevant information, informed the Supreme Council that in this respect the situation in Poland differed from that in Romania. In the old Romania the problem was that the state "...refused to grant the Jews the right of citizenship and the Romanian Jews were protesting against that situation." Referring to Jewish sources, Berthelot went on to claim that "the majority of the Romanian Jews would prefer the omission of Articles 10 and 11 which, although they seem to confer upon them a special status, seemed to place them outside the body of the nation."[62]

The Supreme Council decided to omit the articles in question, but, since in Romania Jews had earlier been denied citizenship (although some had been able to obtain it after a lengthy procedure), a new article was included to change this practice. Romania undertook the obligation to recognize as Romanian citizens those Jews who lived on its territory and who were not citizens of another country (Article 7).

After a few, mostly stylistic, changes to the documents, on December 9 the Romanian delegation, acting on instructions from the Vaida-Voevod government, finally accepted and signed the Austrian peace treaty, the minority protection treaty, and the Bulgarian peace treaty.[63]

Naturally, neither the earlier date of the Austrian peace treaty nor that of the Bulgarian peace treaty was changed by the fact that the Romanian delegates added their signatures to the documents dated and signed by the other parties on September 10 and November 27 respectively. By contrast, the Romanian minority protection treaty is dated December 9, a fact that must be stressed since earlier historical works have often given the date as September 10 or December 5. In the case of the former date, the mistake is due to the existence of a draft treaty dated September 10, prepared at a time when it was still impossible to tell whether or not the Romanian government would sign it together with the Austrian peace treaty. Since by the time the Austrian peace treaty was due to be signed it had become clear that the Romanians would refuse to sign the minority protection agreement, this draft treaty (unlike its Yugoslav counterpart) was put on one side.

As it turned out, the Yugoslav delegation absented itself from the signing ceremony on September 10, and therefore its signature was missing from both the Austrian peace treaty and the minority protection agreement. Nevertheless, the differences did not appear to be so great and consequently the Principal Powers decided to sign the Yugoslav treaty. And although from the Yugoslav point of view the agreement was not binding until December 5, when the Yugoslavs made their declaration, it still bore the date September 10. This confusion must lie behind the fact that in some historical works the Romanian agreement, too, is dated either September 10 or December 5.*

Ion I. C. Brătianu, the influential ex-premier who would later be re-appointed as head of the Romanian government, continued to oppose the minority protection agreement even after it had been signed. At the December 15 meeting of the Romanian Parliament, less than a week after the Vaida-Voevod government had accepted and signed the treaty, Brătianu, now in his capacity as the leader of the opposition, once again set out his arguments against the agreement.[64]

At the time the Romanian minority protection treaty was signed, Bessarabia was still not a *de iure* part of Romania, despite the fact that its entire territory, which had formerly belonged to the Russian Empire, was under the control of the Romanian government. In the introduction of the minority protection agreement, mention was made that the treaty applied "to all inhabitants both of the old Kingdom of Roumania and of the territory added thereto,"[65] but in the treaty, signed on October 28, 1920, recognizing the annexation of Bessarabia to Romania, the Principal Powers still thought it necessary to stress the validity of the minority protection agreement in this territory. The wording of the Bessarabia treaty was such that it could not come into effect until the minority agreement had been enacted.[66]

On December 9, the same day that its members signed the agreement, the United States delegation left the Peace Conference. At 7 pm, immediately after signing the document in the Hotel Crillon, Frank Polk, the head of the delegation; Henry White; and General Tasker Bliss were driven straight to the railway station.[67] This did not mean that subsequently the United

---

* For the text of the Romanian minority protection treaty see Appendix 3.

States was not represented at the meetings of the Supreme Council, merely that its plenipotentiary delegation played no further part in its work. It was Hugh Wallace, the United States ambassador to Paris, who now attended the negotiations, but only as an "observer."[68] Without authority to make decisions himself, Wallace always had to seek Washington's opinion first.

The Greek Minority Protection Agreement and the Exchange of Populations

The minorities committee began to draft the Greek minority protection treaty in the middle of June. On June 18, the text of the first draft was handed to the Greek delegation, and the Supreme Council approved the final text on November 3. Its general articles agreed word-for-word with the earlier documents, but Article 12, the "special" article in the Greek minority protection treaty, demanded the granting of "local autonomy" to the "Kutzo-Vlachs," "in regard to religious, charitable, or scholastic matters."[69] This meant that this minority population—20,000 strong according to the statistics provided by the Greek authorities—was given rights which were tantamount to cultural autonomy.

However, the signing of the Bulgarian peace treaty (this, too, had a minority protection section and was due to be signed on November 27) was not linked to the signing of the Greek minority treaty. Greece's consent to a minority protection agreement to be concluded with the Principal Powers was implied by Article 46 of the Bulgarian peace treaty.

An exchange of populations between Greece and Bulgaria on a voluntary basis was proposed by Eleutherios Venizélos, the Greek prime minister. The Commission on New States and Minorities supported the proposal, but the Supreme Council had reservations about the idea, fearing that it would be difficult to check the degree of voluntariness, and also that, in order to bring about the departure of the minorities, pressure would be exerted upon them. Nevertheless, the Bulgarian government welcomed Venizélos's proposal; negotiations between the two governments now began in the matter, and an agreement was subsequently reached.

Thus, the peace treaty between the Principal Powers and Bulgaria was signed at the same time as the agreement on the exchange of populations between Bulgaria and Greece (November 27, 1919). The Greek minority protection agreement was signed on August 19, 1920, shortly after the Treaty of Sèvres with Turkey (August 8, 1920).

The Turkish revolution led by Mustapha Kemal (Atatürk) refused to accept the Sèvres treaty and managed to have it replaced by a more favorable one. The final Turkish peace treaty, signed in Lausanne in 1923, was accompanied by another agreement, one concluded between Greece and Turkey and dealing with an exchange of populations. However, this exchange of populations was to be compulsory, since in the tense circumstances which then prevailed, minority protection could not be guaranteed in any other way. Approximately 1,500,000 Greek nationals from the Izmir region were now uprooted, and about 500,000 Turks were uprooted from Greece.

Thus, in dealings with minorities, the practice of exchanging populations, both in its voluntary and its mandatory form, was introduced in the years following World War I, although it achieved wider acceptance only after World War II.

In 1918, the starting point in drafting the minority protection agreements was that, irrespective of the change of borders, citizens should be secure in their fundamental rights, human and minority, in their own homelands. The principle of a person's right to live in his homeland regardless of border alterations was manifest in a number of ways in the obligations—in the minority protection agreements as well as in the peace treaties—undertaken by the states concerned.

The Minority Protection Passages
in the Hungarian Peace Treaty

Of all the peace treaties relating to East Central Europe, the one causing the greatest difficulties was probably the peace treaty with Hungary. The fact that Hungary adopted a different approach raised problems from the very beginning. Conceptually, Austria and Bulgaria followed a "national" line, as did their opponents

—at least as far as the basic principles and first premises were concerned. This was true despite the fact that the economic and transportation arguments which stressed the need for the economic rehabilitation of the countries concerned invariably pointed beyond ethnic-national lines. And although the demands of the new Allied states were never in harmony with the national principle they professed at the Peace Conference, they were in the same "language." By contrast, official Hungarian policy rejected the redrawing of the political map in the Carpathian Basin on a national basis, and was prepared to accept only the historical approach. The scope of the present work does not permit a more detailed investigation of this issue; for present purposes, we shall have to content ourselves with emphasizing that in Hungarian thinking at this time the "national" principle was closely connected to the geographical unity represented by the Carpathian Basin and to the historical character of the state ruling it. For the Hungarians, Hungarian "national" demands, which were widely believed to be just and fair, were not confined to those areas inhabited by ethnic Hungarians, but covered the entire territory of historical Hungary, the old multinational state. Consequently, Hungarian public opinion was unable to accept the disintegration into its ethno-national components of the thousand-year-old state; this was regarded as being directly contrary to Hungary's national interests.

In 1918, following the collapse of the Habsburg Monarchy, a liberal democratic government was established in Hungary under the leadership of Count Mihály Károlyi. This continued with the earlier approach and, consequently, encountered very serious difficulties. Regarding the loss of the ethnically non-Hungarian territories as a violation of Hungarian "national" interests, the new régime was unable to accept it. However, as long as the Czech and the Romanian armies confined their advance to areas populated largely by Slovaks and Romanians, the situation was more or less stable. But when the armies of occupation reached areas with Hungarian majorities (this first happened in Transylvania), Hungarian defiance and opposition—now national in the true sense of the word—finally flared up. The Supreme Council of the Peace Conference, unable to deploy neutral forces to separate the opposing armies, ordered the Hungarian defenders to move further and further back. The Hungarian public became infuriated by this, and the infamous "Vix Note" was the last straw. However, since the Károlyi government lacked broad domestic support, it was unable to stand up against the Peace Conference's more extreme demands. Armed resistance was attempted by the 1919 Hungarian Soviet Republic, a régime which sought to link up with Soviet Russia. However, the military superiority of the neighboring states, which oriented themselves towards the Peace Conference, put an end to this.

The situation which followed the overthrow of the Soviet Republic, which had been defiant in its dealings with Paris, proved equally unsuitable for the conclusion of a peace treaty with Hungary. With much of its territory now occupied by Romanian troops, Hungary was unable to set up contact with the Peace Conference. First of all, the reluctant Romanians had to be made to withdraw, and the murderous activities of the counter-revolutionary officers' detachments had to give way to a more liberal order, one which was acceptable to Western public opinion. It was not until several months later that the Paris Peace Conference could invite Hungary: on December 1, 1919 the Supreme Council called on the Hungarian government to send a delegation to receive the peace terms which had been decided.[70]

The Hungarian peace delegation, led by Count Albert Apponyi, arrived in Paris (or, more precisely, in Neuilly) on January 6, 1920.

The draft treaty was handed to the delegation on January 15; the text followed that of the earlier treaties with regard to structure and order. Of the treaty's 364 articles, 290 were identical to those in the German and the Austrian treaties. In the matter of border changes, the frontiers proposed differed from those finally adopted only to the extent that the town of Sopron and its vicinity were awarded to Austria and not Hungary. The size of the Hungarian army was limited to 35,000 men; furthermore, Hungary was ordered to pay reparations, the exact amount of which was to be specified later. (As it turned out, the sum eventually decided upon was not unduly extortionate.)

As in the case of the German and Austrian delegations, the Hungarian delegation was also given the opportunity to express its views concerning the draft treaty. Thus, on January 16, 1920,

Apponyi was allowed to appear in front of the Supreme Council, accompanied by some other members of his delegation. In his speech, Apponyi listed the arguments for preserving the old territorial integrity. Fortunately, this was not the end of the matter; David Lloyd George, the British prime minister, asked Apponyi to estimate the number of Hungarians who would be separated from Hungary if the proposed border changes were implemented.

From Lloyd George's question and the subsequent arguments it became clear that the only way for Hungary to proceed would have been to follow the German and Austrian example and to ask for revisions to the draft on the basis of the ethnic-language principle, rather than to insist to the last on the old territorial integrity. And although some of Budapest's reply notes and declarations indicated a certain recognition of this, the official Hungarian view concerning the draft treaty remained one of unwavering adherence to pre-1918 borders.

Unlike the Austrian politicians, the Hungarian leaders were unable to switch from the historical to the national principle at the critical moment. Regardless of whether a Hungarian policy similar to the German or the Austrian would have achieved a territorial settlement more favorable to Hungary, it would nevertheless have been important that the delegation's criticism of the draft treaty took the form of a realistic and national opposition, instead of a hopeless insistence on the preservation of the historical frontiers.

After twice extending the deadline, the Peace Conference expected the Hungarian reply notes by mid-February at the latest. On May 6, the Hungarian peace delegation received the final text, now with minor alterations and with the stipulation that the Hungarian government must give an answer by May 26. Hungary's reply indicating acceptance, inevitable in the circumstances, arrived before the appointed date.

It was not in the sanctioning of the disintegration of historical Hungary that the harshness of the peace terms resided. Rather, it lay in the fact that nearly three million Hungarians, needlessly and without justification, were stripped of their Hungarian citizenship. The need to separate the various nationalities living in the Carpathian Basin could never have warranted this, since the overwhelming majority of the Hungarians thus detached (with the exception of the Szeklers) all lived in compact blocs adjacent to the main body of the Hungarian people. The Treaty of Trianon, therefore, not only sanctioned the disintegration of the old, multinational Hungary, but it also effected the unnecessary division of the Hungarian people. In this way the treaty seriously violated the national principle which was to serve, on paper at least, as the basis for the region's rearrangement.

Although such a blatant violation of the national principle was by no means unique in the re-ordering of the new state system in East Central Europe (one has only to think of the millions of Austrian Germans transferred to Czechoslovakia and Italy, or the millions of Ukrainians and Byelorussians ending up in Poland), there could be, however, no justification for such a painful and unnecessary development.

*

Section VI of the draft treaty, handed to the Hungarian delegation on January 15, 1920, contained seven points dealing with the minority protection obligations Hungary was expected to undertake.* These were word-for-word the same as those comprising the section contained in the Austrian peace treaty, which had already been signed.[71] In the Hungarian minority protection obligations, essentially the same general obligations were formulated as in its Polish, Czechoslovak, and Romanian counterparts. In its reply note of February 20, the Hungarian delegation accepted the seven points without critical comment: "The Hungarian Delegation regard it as their duty to observe that the dispositions of the Articles in question (54-60) are in agreement with the ideas that served as the basis of Hungarian legislation in these matters, and correspond to the provisions of our laws now in force.[72]"

Although the chapters formulating the minority protection obligations in the Austrian and Hungarian peace treaties were almost identical, there was an important difference. The Austrian peace treaty incorporated the Czechoslovak, Yugoslav, and Romanian minority protection obligations—in the form of a reference to the agreement by these states to conclude such treaties with

---

* See Appendix 4.

the Principal Powers.[73] As already mentioned, this was the reason for the eruption of the dispute at the plenary meeting of May 31. By contrast, the draft of the Hungarian peace treaty contained no such references. The Hungarian reply note expressed astonishment over the omission:

> But the Hungarian Delegation cannot conceal their astonishment at the fact that the stipulations contained in Articles 51, 57 and 60 of the Treaty of Peace concluded between the Allied and Associated Powers and Austria referring to the duty of the Serb-Croat-Slovene State, of the Czechoslovak State, and of Roumania to consent to the insertion in a Treaty of such provisions for the protection of the interests of those inhabitants who differ from the majority of the population in race, language, or religion, as may be deemed proper by the Principal Powers, are completely missing from the draft treaty handed to the Hungarian Delegation.[74]

The Supreme Council of the Peace Conference acknowledged the Hungarian comment.

The reply note to the comment made by the Hungarian delegation was signed by Alexandre Millerand, the new head of the French government, on behalf of the Allied and Associated Powers. As this May 6 answer explained, the Hungarian peace treaty —unlike the Austrian—did not include the passages on minority protection in the neighboring countries because in the meantime minority protection agreements had been concluded with the three states concerned. However, as at that time only the Czechoslovak treaty had been ratified, the subsequent inclusion of the relevant passages in the treaties with the Serb-Croat-Slovene state and Romania was indeed justified.[75] At the same time, the Peace Conference rejected the detailed Hungarian request (Accompanying Note No. XXIII), the substance of which was a request to extend minority protection in the neighboring states to include the assurance of religious and cultural autonomy.[76] With reference to those Hungarians who were to become minorities in the neighboring states, Millerand's accompanying letter, also dated May 6, said: "The Treaties for the protection of minorities already signed by Roumania and the Serb-Croat-Slovene State and ratified by Czecho-Slovakia guarantee their interests completely."[77]

Thus, the Hungarian peace treaty, signed on June 4, 1920 in the Trianon Palace at Versailles, expressly referred (in Articles 44 and 47) to the internationally-guaranteed minority protection obligations of Yugoslavia and Romania, and the accompanying letter from Millerand referred to the minority protection agreements concluded with the two countries, and to the minority protection treaty already ratified by Czechoslovakia, suggesting that they fully guaranteed the interests of the Hungarian minorities who had passed under the rule of the three countries in question.

The measures concomitant with the Hungarian peace treaty clearly show that the Principal Powers regarded minority protection as an organic part of the new state system. When the borders were redrawn in favor of the successor states, economic and strategic considerations took precedence over the ethnic principle and over the doctrine of self-determination (the leaders of the Principal Powers were united in this approach, although Lloyd George was less committed to it than Clemenceau). Nevertheless, in the state system thus established these leaders did make minority protection an organic element. The Paris peace treaties and the protection of minorities formed a package for the postwar rearrangement of the Carpathian Basin, as did the re-alignment of states and internationally-guaranteed minority protection in the whole of the East Central European belt.

The Peace Conference required Hungary to accept and recognize its new boundaries, but at the same time—and in the same document—guaranteed international protection for the minority rights of those Hungarians who now constituted minorities outside Hungary's borders. The peace system following World War I integrated international treatment of the two problems.

The internationally-guaranteed assurance of minority rights was not restricted to civic equality to be realized in all fields. It created a basis, a point of departure. The principle of civic equality was extended to equality before the law, to equal access to public authorities, and to equality of opportunity in employment. It also applied to the unrestricted use of one's mother-tongue.

Article 7 of the treaties with Czechoslovakia and Yugoslavia, and Article 8 of the Romanian treaty clearly and unequivocally stated:

> No restriction shall be imposed on the free use by any national of any language in private intercourse, in commerce, in religion, in the press or in publications of any kind, or at public meetings.

Internationally-sanctioned minority rights also included freedom of schooling in the mother-tongue, formulated in Article 8 of the Czechoslovak and Yugoslav treaties, and in Article 9 of the Romanian treaty:

> ... they [the minorities] shall have an equal right to establish, manage, and control at their own expense, charitable, religious, and social institutions, schools and other educational establishments with the right to use their own language and exercise their religion freely therein.

In addition, minority rights protection obligated the states to set up schools in areas inhabited by minorities which used the minority language, and to finance these schools or institutions from their budgets on a proportional basis.* These minority rights had to be granted by Czechoslovakia, Yugoslavia, and Romania on one side, and by Hungary and Austria on the other. This meant that every state in the Danube region—whether "winner" or "loser"—was obliged to ensure these minority rights under international supervision.

Neither the new and enlarged states, nor Hungary nor Austria disputed the justification and need for these rights. Even the initial opposition on the part of Yugoslavia and Romania was more or less confined to the objection that these treaties had been imposed on them and were guaranteed and supervised by states that had no similar obligations. Thus, only the need for international guarantee and supervision was disputed.

---

* See Article 8 of the Czechoslovak and Yugoslav, and 9 of the Romanian, treaty.

Czechoslovakia had incorporated these rights in its *corpus iuris* before it signed the document accepting the international obligations. The leaders of Yugoslavia and Romania had, on their own initiative, reiterated the intention of their respective states to ensure minority rights. At that time not even Romania, the most insistent objector to international supervision, questioned the inclusion in the sphere of minority rights the right of the minorities to use their own languages and their own schools. Nor did Romania object to the minorities' right to foster their own cultures and religions, or to full civic equality. Moreover, Romania did not oppose cultural autonomy for the Szekler and Saxon enclaves in Transylvania.

Thus, the organic integration of the new boundaries with the guarantee of minority rights—as a structure ensuring peace for the peoples in the Danube region—was no longer disputed; the polemics were directed merely at the need for international control.

Finally, it should be emphasized that during the 1920s heated discussions about the interpretation of minority rights took place throughout Europe, and, therefore, at the League of Nations also. These discussions were not about whether the minorities were entitled to the full range of minority rights: that they were so entitled was widely accepted by the parties concerned. The debate centered around the issue of whether the right to autonomy—be it cultural, political, or territorial—should be comprehensively guaranteed and internationally supervised. The largest part of the minorities, together with those nations which had large populations living as minorities in the neighboring states, were of the opinion that the right to autonomy belonged among minority rights. By contrast, those states which contained large minority populations rejected this claim. The debates on the interpretation of minority rights during the 1920s were confined first of all to this problem. It follows from the above, therefore, that the minority protection treaties concluded after World War I stipulated the minimum special human rights which the minorities could justly claim under all circumstances.

Chapter 4
The International Guarantees in Practice

In the previous chapters we examined the work performed by the Peace Conference in the interests of the minorities living in the reorganized East Central European belt, and in support of the internationally-guaranteed protection of their rights. Nevertheless, the Peace Conference, when drawing and sanctioning the new frontiers, could only lay the foundations of minority protection. Through its various legal constructs (minority protection treaties, the minority protection sections of the peace treaties, and the Covenant of the League of Nations), the Peace Conference created the framework for the minorities' international protection, but the task of setting this protection in motion and developing concrete procedures was to fall to the League of Nations itself.

The Declaration of the League of Nations' Guarantee

On June 28, 1919, the Covenant of the League of Nations was signed by the victorious powers and by the countries attending the Peace Conference. The governments of several neutral countries were given to understand that their countries, too, could become founding members simply by declaring their intention to join the League. But the signature of the Covenant was not tantamount to the putting into force of the League: ratification of the Covenant by the signatory states (and, most importantly, by the Principal Powers at the Peace Conference) was also necessary.

This ratification took place in a rather unusual way. The text of the League of Nations' Covenant was also incorporated in the peace treaties. When the German treaty was signed—this was the first to be signed—its opening section was reserved for the text of the League of Nations' Covenant. The arrangement was retained for all the other peace treaties. Therefore, ratification of the German peace treaty also meant the acceptance of the League of

Nations' Covenant, and no separate procedure was needed. The concluding section of the German peace treaty stated that the agreement would only become operative when representatives of at least three of the Principal Powers, together with the representatives of Germany, received the ratification document in Paris. Thus, on the day the German peace treaty was ratified (January 10, 1920), the League of Nations could begin its work.[1] At the time it had as its members those Allied and Associated Powers which had ratified the Covenant, that is, the German peace treaty. (The first chapter of the German treaty was the text of the Covenant.)

Since the United States was not among the ratifying countries, it did not become a member. To become members with immediate effect, those neutral countries which had been invited to join only needed to declare their intention to do so within two months. After this, a two-thirds majority within the General Assembly was necessary for the admission of any new applicants. By 1923, following the admission of the neutral countries and several "loser" states (Hungary, for example, joined the organization in 1922), the number of countries belonging to the League of Nations had reached fifty-four; by this time every European country except Germany and the Soviet Union had become a member.[2]

On January 10, 1920 the League of Nations began its work via the Secretariat. Article 6 of the Covenant regulated the work of the Secretariat, but it also invested the Council with the right to appoint the Secretary, provided that his appointment was approved by a majority in the General Assembly. Even so, the Secretariat was able to begin its work before the Council and the General Assembly was first convened: the Appendix of the Covenant appointed Britain's Sir Eric Drummond to serve as Secretary until such time as the Council proposed its candidate.[3] (Drummond was subsequently confirmed in this post by the first General Assembly.)

The minority protection treaties and the relevant chapters of the peace treaties, however, referred the entire problem of minority protection to the jurisdiction of the Council, not to that of the Secretariat. According to Article 4 of the Covenant, the Council was to consist partly of representatives of the Principal Allied and Associated Powers (the United States, Britain, France,

Italy, and Japan, which were all to be permanent members of the Council), and partly of the representatives of four other member-states, which were to be chosen periodically by the General Assembly. Until the selection of these four states by the General Assembly, Belgium, Brazil, Spain, and Greece were nominated to serve on the Council. In this way the Council, too, was able to commence work before the first session of the General Assembly. Obviously, the ratification of the Covenant by the nine countries on the Council was a precondition for calling the Council into session. As the United States did not, in fact, become a member of the League of Nations, in the first few years the Council had four permanent and four elected members.

In 1922, the third General Assembly voted to raise the number of elected members to six. The seventh General Assembly, held in 1926, admitted Germany to the League of Nations and awarded it a permanent seat on the Council. During the same General Assembly, the number of elected members was raised to nine; the system of representation was also changed: from this time on, three new members were elected every three years, each for a period of three years.

Incidentally, the Covenant of the League of Nations required that the first session of the Council be called by the President of the United States, although the United States was not even a member. Still, this did not prevent the U.S. head of state from performing this duty, and thus the first session of the Council was called by President Woodrow Wilson, to be held in Paris on January 16, 1920. Naturally, the session was not attended by a representative of the United States, as the latter did not ratify the Covenant.[4]

The Council held ten sessions in its first year and afterwards was convened four to five times annually. It was immediately confronted with the problems of minority protection, the international guarantee of which the League of Nations had taken upon itself. First of all, the Council had to address the anomaly represented by the fact that the agreements between the Principal Powers and the new and enlarged states of East Central Europe (Poland, Czechoslovakia, Romania, Yugoslavia, and Greece) not only listed the rights to which the local minorities were entitled, but also entrusted the guaranteeing of these rights to the League of Nations, an organization which had no legal existence when these agreements were concluded. Similarly, the peace treaties signed with the "loser" states of the region (Austria, Hungary, Bulgaria, and Turkey) also incorporated minority rights to be guaranteed by the League of Nations. In addition to the anomaly outlined above, the Council had to face another problem: the treaties listed definite rights, but contained little information about how these were to be guaranteed in practice.

In all nine treaties (the five minority protection treaties and the four peace treaties) it was explicitly stated that the granting of minority rights was the "international obligation" of the given state, and that compliance with these rights was "placed under the international guarantee of the League of Nations." (See Article 12 of the Polish treaty, Article 14 of the Czechoslovak, Article 12 of the Romanian, Article 11 of the Serb-Croat-Slovene, Article 16 of the Greek, Article 69 of the Austrian, Article 60 of the Hungarian, Article 57 of the Bulgarian and Article 44 of the Turkish [Lausanne] treaty.[5])

While some definite information concerning the content of the League of Nations guarantee was contained in the articles listed above, it was hardly sufficient. Nevertheless, it did provide a starting point for working out the details of the international guarantee in practice. The main starting points could be summed up as follows:

1. Only the Council (and not the General Assembly) of the League of Nations could modify the minority protection articles; and only a simple majority (rather than a unanimous decision) was needed in the Council for the introduction of changes to the articles.

2. Every member of the Council was entitled to call the attention of the Council to the violation or to the danger of violation of the obligations undertaken by the signatories of the treaties. (Therefore, only the members of the *Council* enjoyed this right.)

3. If such a violation, or danger of violation, was established after a member had called the Council's attention to it, the Council could take "proper and effective action."

4. If a difference of opinion emerged between any member of the Council and a state in question with regard to minority rights or the interpretation of facts, then, according to Article 14 of the

Covenant, it had to be viewed as a dispute of international concern.

5. Such a dispute could, at the request of any Council Member, be submitted for judgment by the Permanent Court of International Justice; the decision of this body would be final, and would have the same force and validity as any resolution passed in observance of Article 13 of the League of Nations' Covenant.

This much was contained, therefore, in the minority protection treaties, and in the minority protection sections of the peace treaties in connection with the League of Nations guarantee. Lacking in substance and in concreteness, it was nevertheless adequate as a point of departure. Evidently, it was the Council of the League of Nations which would play a crucial part in the practical implementation of the international guarantee. It also became clear that the initiative of the Council members would be of paramount importance. The active support of a Council member was needed if an alleged violation of the minority protection treaties was to be classified as a dispute of international concern. In such a case the rules and the procedures were to be the same as the general rules and procedures described by the Covenant of the League of Nations for handling any conflict emerging between nations.

Without disputing that the passages dealing with the international guarantee contained important guidelines and statements on a general level, we can see that they said very little about concrete procedural matters. This deficiency is explained by the fact that the Covenant of the League of Nations, which did not mention the protection of the minorities at all, was drafted before the drawing up of the minority protection treaties and the minority protection sections of the peace treaties. When it was agreed that the treaties would be guaranteed by the League of Nations, the actual measures stipulated in the treaties had to be harmonized with the text of the already-existing Covenant.

The League of Nations' Covenant, therefore, could not contain a guarantee of the minority protection treaties, since it was formulated before the treaties were drafted. However, such a guarantee was mentioned in the minority protection treaties. Consequently, it became necessary for the League of Nations to eliminate this loophole in the law and undertake the guarantee as soon as it began to operate. Of course, a legal consistency between the corresponding documents can be discerned, especially in the case of the peace treaties, since the signatories to these were, by and large, the founding members of the League of Nations. As for the minority protection treaties, these were concluded by the Principal Powers: the same states that became the permanent members of the League of Nations' Council. This legal overlap was, however, no substitute for the undertaking of proper legal obligations.

Although every member-state was required to have its international treaties "registered" with the League of Nations, this alone was unable to solve the problem mentioned above. Countries which were not members were obviously not bound by this regulation, although they, too, could have their treaties registered with the League of Nations if they so desired. Members of the League undertook not to conclude international agreements which were irreconcilable with the Covenant (Article 20). The obligation to have every international agreement registered with the Secretariat (Article 18) followed from this. However, by itself, registration could not remove the said legal anomaly, if for no other reason than the sheer number of treaties registered. During the lifetime of the League, more than 4,700 treaties were registered, the official publication of these required 200 volumes.[6]

Nevertheless, a procedure to handle the aforementioned problem was finally developed whereby the Council guaranteed each minority protection treaty, and minority protection section of each peace treaty, in separate resolutions. Subsequent agreements concluded between two or more states and containing minority protection clauses would not automatically be guaranteed by the League of Nations. In each such case the League of Nations guarantee had to be declared separately.

The first declaration took place on February 13, 1920, during the February session of the Council. On this occasion, the relevant sections of the Polish minority protection treaty were placed under the League of Nations' guarantee.[7]

Similarly, on October 22, 1920 the Council guaranteed the minority protection sections of the Austrian peace treaty (enacted on July 16) and those of the Bulgarian peace agreement (enacted on August 9) in two separate resolutions. A month later, on November 29, the Czechoslovak, Yugoslav, and Romanian minority protection agreements received the League of Nations' guarantee. (The first two minority protection agreements were enacted on July 26; the Romanian treaty was put into effect on September 4.)

The minority protection sections of the Hungarian peace treaty (Articles 54 to 60) were placed under League of Nations' guarantee on August 30, 1921. (The treaty itself was enacted on July 26, 1921.) In the case of the Greek minority protection treaty and the minority protection sections of the Lausanne peace treaty with Turkey, the League guarantee was given on September 26, 1924.

Additional League Guarantees

In addition to the treaties drawn up by the Peace Conference, there were some other minority protection accords that the League of Nations guaranteed. On December 15, 1920, the first General Assembly passed a resolution to the effect that if Albania, the Baltic States and the Caucasian states were to be admitted to the League of Nations, the minorities there would also need to be protected.[8]

This resolution was passed by the General Assembly on the recommendation of Committee V, which had been formed to process the applications of additional states wishing to join the League. During the first General Assembly, this committee appointed a sub-committee to clarify certain fundamental questions. The aforementioned recommendation was worked out by this sub-committee, and was subsequently endorsed by the General Assembly.

Here we should say a few words about the committees formed to help the work of the General Assemblies, since we shall hear more about them in later discussions. The annual meeting of the League of Nations' General Assembly always opened and closed with a plenary session. Six committees were formed to assist the work of the General Assembly, in the same way that parliamentary committees help the work of a parliament. Each member-state delegated one representative to each committee. But although the committees were high-level bodies, they were not empowered to make decisions. They presented their recommendations to the

General Assembly during the plenary sessions, and these recommendations became resolutions only when the General Assembly endorsed them.[9]

The minority protection issue was discussed, mostly on a theoretical level but sometimes also in concrete terms, in Committee VI, or the Political Committee, as it was also called. It was this committee that made most of the recommendations regarding the protection of the minorities—recommendations that were then submitted to the General Assembly.

Following the endorsement of a resolution by the plenary meeting of the General Assembly, the governments of Finland and Albania declared their willingness to cooperate with the League of Nations on minority protection issues. On the strength of these declarations, the General Assembly admitted the two countries to membership of the League on December 17, 1920. This was followed by negotiations between the Council and the Finnish and Albanian governments in the matter of minority rights.

The negotiations with the Finnish government ended during the June 1921 session of the Council. The Finnish government announced the legislative measures and the concrete procedures by which the rights of Finland's minorities—mostly Swedes— were to be fully guaranteed. In addition, the Finnish leaders declared their intention to preserve both the legislation and the procedures in the future.

The Council acknowledged this declaration, and, in fact, found it unnecessary to place Finland's minority laws under League of Nations' guarantee. The Council held different views with regard to the Aaland Islands, an archipelago under Finnish rule. These islands had belonged to Sweden until 1809, when they were ceded to Russia. After the declaration of Finnish independence (1917), control over these islands had passed from Russia to Finland. The census of 1910 had put the population of the Aaland Islands at 21,356, of whom 92.5 percent—i.e. all but 895 persons—were Swedish-speaking.[10]

The Finnish Parliament passed a law concerning autonomy for the islands as early as May 7, 1920. The League of Nations required that Finland and Sweden reach agreement over the substance of this; a six-article-long treaty was signed by the two states on June 27, 1921.[11] The Council placed the treaty under the League of Nations' guarantee on the day of its signature, by adding a seventh article which proclaimed the guarantee.[12]

The Finnish example serves to show, therefore, that neither unilateral minority protection measures, nor bilateral protection agreements were automatically guaranteed by the League. Such a guarantee required a separate decision and separate procedure. This meant that minority rights in general—in the case of both domestic legislation and international agreements—constituted a larger set than did the minority rights guaranteed by the League of Nations.

The negotiations with the Albanian government were somewhat prolonged, owing to the Greek government's insistence on the inclusion in the Albanian minority protection treaty of certain passages that the Albanian government was unable to accept. (Greece happened to be one of the elected members of the Council.) One such demand was that any Greek government report on the violations of minority rights in Albania be regarded as originating from a member of the Council, regardless of whether Greece was still a member of this body. This was rejected by the majority of the Council members.

Finally, on October 2, 1921, the Albanian government was able to submit to the Council a declaration on the protection of the minorities in Albania. The content of the declaration, which consisted of seven articles, was essentially the same as the minority protection treaties formulated by the Peace Conference, or the minority protection sections of the peace treaties.[13] The Albanian Parliament ratified the declaration on February 17, 1922, and, accordingly, the guarantee of the League of Nations came into effect.[14]

The next minority protection obligation to be guaranteed by the League of Nations concerned Upper Silesia. Sovereignty over this territory should have been settled by a plebiscite held on March 20, 1921, but the results showed that only in certain parts of Upper Silesia did the population vote unequivocally in favor of joining either Poland or Germany. Since in the rest of Upper Silesia no clear decision emerged, it was not possible to divide the region satisfactorily on the basis of the plebiscite. Eventually, on

October 20, 1921 the territory was divided between Germany and Poland according to a decision by the Conference of Ambassadors acting on behalf of the Peace Conference. At the same time, the two governments concerned were required to begin negotiations in order to settle the minority problem to the mutual satisfaction of both parties.

On May 17, 1922, the negotiations between Germany and Poland ended successfully and a treaty formulating the rights of the minorities in divided Upper Silesia was signed. Articles 64 to 178 inclusive contained mutually recognized minority rights, largely based on the principles of the Polish minority protection treaty, although in considerably more detail. This treaty, or more precisely its sections dealing with the protection of minorities, was placed under the guarantee of the League of Nations.[15]

Estonia, Latvia and Lithuania, the three Baltic States, were admitted to membership in the League of Nations on September 22, 1921, at the time of the second General Assembly. Previously, each of the three governments had signed a declaration to the effect that, in accordance with the General Assembly's resolution of December 15, 1920, it was willing to hold talks with the Council in order to determine its concrete minority protection obligations.[16]

Next, the Council appointed one of its members, Brazil, to begin negotiations with the governments of the three countries to prepare for the necessary declarations regarding the rights of minorities. The declaration of the Lithuanian government was accepted first, on May 12, 1922. The Latvian declaration was read at the July 7, 1922 session of the Council. A similar declaration was made by the representative of the Estonian government on September 17, 1923. The content of these declarations basically followed the content of the minority protection agreements guaranteed earlier by the League.[17]

The League of Nations extended its guarantee to one more minority protection obligation. On May 8, 1924, the Principal Powers of the Peace Conference concluded an agreement with the Lithuanian government concerning the union of Lithuania and the *Memelland.* (After the war the Memel region, which had formerly belonged to Germany, was placed under League of Nations supervision.) The treaty also had minority protection aspects (Articles 11 and 27). These were placed under the guarantee of the League on September 27, 1924, the day the agreement was ratified.[18]

The Memel treaty completes the list of treaties containing minority protection obligations guaranteed by the League of Nations.

There were numerous other international treaties guaranteeing minority rights in East Central Europe in addition to those placed under the guarantee of the League of Nations. An example of an international treaty not guaranteed by the League, in spite of its bearing on minority rights, was the agreement signed between Latvia and Lithuania on May 14, 1921. In Article 13 of the agreement, each country guaranteed the free establishment and development of the national and cultural associations of the other's people living within its borders.[19] Also, several agreements were concluded between Yugoslavia and Italy which touched upon the minority problem (Rapallo, November 12, 1920; Rome, October 23, 1922; and Nettuno, July 20, 1925).[20] In the East Central European belt, additional treaties were signed which affected the national minorities; these mostly granted rights similar to those listed in the minority protection treaties guaranteed by the League. This process indicates the positive and permeative effect the League of Nations' policies had on the region with regard to the protection of minorities.

In a number of states, domestic legislation actually ensured broader rights for the minorities than was demanded by the internationally-guaranteed agreements. Probably the best example of a country with such legislation was Estonia.

The Estonian government declared that the country's constitution and laws ensured for the minorities those rights which the principles of international minority protection demanded. (This was the declaration placed under the guarantee of the League of Nations on September 17, 1923.) Accordingly, the minorities living in Estonia were guaranteed enjoyment of the same rights that had been laid down in the minority protection treaties.

Later, however, the Estonian government went on to grant additional rights to the minorities. In February 1925, the Estonian Parliament passed a law conferring cultural autonomy on the minorities. In line with this, each national minority became a legal entity and took over the fostering of its culture, together with rights which had previously belonged to the central and local authorities—for example, the running of schools, libraries, theaters, and museums. These cultural bodies were self-governing and could issue decrees on matters belonging to their sphere of authority. They could also levy taxes; in any event the state was obliged to allocate a proportionate amount of the central budget to them.[21]

The aforementioned examples serve to illustrate the fact that *the minority obligations guaranteed by the League of Nations were not regarded as the last word on the protection of minorities*. From the statements made by the Council and by the General Assembly, it is clear that *the League of Nations encouraged, both in Europe and in the other continents, the creation of similar legal guarantees, maintaining that the minority rights guaranteed by the League constituted only the minimum such rights*.

The question directly following from the above is why the Peace Conference and the League of Nations did not extend the system of guarantees to the minorities living outside the East Central European zone, rejecting the idea of making minority protection a general obligation, although the League itself recommended that all states ensure similar rights for their minorities. What makes this question all the more interesting is the fact that some of the countries bound by the minority protection agreements pushed through by the Peace Conference continued to resent the discriminatory nature of the League's minority protection policies. From their arguments it appeared as though they were not so much against minority rights in general as the form they took. This was resented as being humiliating and even constituting an infringement of national sovereignty. It was also seen as binding only certain countries to the protection of their minorities, when in fact the right of supervising compliance with the obligations was reserved to countries which had undertaken no such obligations themselves.

The cause of minority protection was not championed by the Peace Conference and its creation, the League of Nations, for "its own sake." These bodies did not claim· (nor did they deny) that minority rights should constitute fundamental human rights. The protection of minorities was only one element in a system of guarantees introduced to ensure international peace in a region experiencing radical changes. In the introduction to the Covenant of the League of Nations, it is unequivocally stated that the League of Nations was established "in order to promote the co-operation of the nations and realize international peace and security."[22] As mentioned earlier, the minority problem was thought to constitute a serious threat to the stability of East Central Europe.

Since, as a result of the re-alignment of states in Europe, millions of people were now forced to live the life of minorities, their protection became a vitally important element in the preservation of peace. In fact, it was in this region that conditions made the international guarantees necessary. This was particularly manifest in Wilson's speech at the plenary meeting of the Peace Conference held on May 31, 1919, as well as in Clemenceau's letter accompanying the Polish minority treaty. We have already seen that on several occasions the various bodies of the League of Nations recommended that all member-states develop a similar system of minority protection. Nevertheless, the international guarantee system was reserved for East Central Europe, as it was here that the worsening of minority conflicts posed the greatest threat to world peace.

In the reorganized East Central European belt during the years after World War I, the number of people living as members of a national minority was roughly thirty million. As already mentioned, most of these people became minorities as a direct consequence of the post-war rearrangement. To complicate matters further, many of these minorities possessed an advanced culture and were highly aware of their national and ethnic identities.

Although minority problems existed everywhere in the world, during the 1920s only the conflicts involving these European minorities could threaten the world with another conflagration.

While the League's reluctance to extend internationally-guaranteed minority protection throughout the world could still cause disagreements, in light of the above the restriction of League of Nations guarantees to specific cases does seem to have been justified.

The Guarantee Procedure[23]

In 1920, the first year of its existence, the League of Nations undertook to guarantee the minority protection sections of six different treaties. At the same time, clarification of the guarantee procedure became necessary, since the treaties themselves said nothing more in this respect than that in the event of violation the Council be empowered to take "proper and effective action."

The League of Nations worked out the details of its guarantee procedure between 1920 and 1923. Since the treaties always referred to the Council members in connection with the obligations and duties of the guarantee procedure, the implementation of the procedures was assigned primarily to the Council, although the active participation of Committee VI of the General Assembly, as well as of the General Assembly itself, also was required later.

The Council appointed the foreign minister of one of its permanent members, Italy, to work out a proposal and to submit it to the Council. By this arrangement, the Council established the protocol of regarding one of the Council members as the *Rapporteur* of minority problems. The Italian foreign minister, Tittoni, who served in this capacity in 1920 and 1921, was replaced first by Belgium's Hymans and then by Britain's Arthur J. Balfour.[24] Instead of handling specific cases, the mechanism for which will be shown later, the *Rapporteur* was involved with the theoretical and procedural aspects of the Council's responsibilities concerning minority protection.

Tittoni's report was discussed and approved by the Council when it met in Brussels on October 22, 1920.[25] This meeting established the guarantee procedure to be employed in practice. The report, and the resolution adopted on the basis of it, became the most important elements in the League's minority protection activities and for this reason they deserve to be examined in some detail.*

---

* For the complete text, see Appendix 5.

Tittoni's report took as its point of departure those articles of the treaties which dealt with the guarantees. After a detailed discussion of the content of the articles, the report summed up in three points what was really meant by "League of Nations' guarantees" with regard to minority rights. These were as follows:

1. Any modification to the minority rights set down in the treaties, or to the signatories' obligations to comply with them, would require a majority vote in the League of Nations' Council.

2. At all times the League needed to establish whether the laws and regulations serving the protection of the minorities were being observed. (Incidentally, the information service provided by the Secretariat of the League grew out of this obligation.)

3. The Council was required to take action in every case in which the minority protection obligations undertaken in the treaties were violated, or when the threat of such violation had emerged.

The Tittoni report went into some detail on this third point. It explained that the countries represented on the Council would have the right and the duty to call the Council's attention to actual, or threatened, violation of the minority protection agreements. This, however, did not exclude the possibility that the minorities themselves might report breeches of the agreements to the Council in form of petitions; in fact, the minorities should be encouraged to do this. But by itself such a petition would not warrant the launching of a "legal procedure;" this would require the active support of at least one Council member. Therefore, only a Council member could set the guarantee mechanism in motion.

This issue had already been debated in 1919, at the June 6, 7, and 16 meetings of the Council of Four. Then, three options had been considered, namely that:

1. Any member of the League of Nations should be able to activate the guarantee mechanism;

2. Only a Council member should be able to activate it, or;

3. Only a permanent member of the Council should be able to do so.

During the debate, Wilson had expressed the opinion that every member of the League of Nations should be given this right. At that time the decision had been made—at the proposal of Lloyd

George and Clemenceau—that the opinion of the leaders of the Allied countries to be obligated by the planned minority protection agreements (that is, Beneš, Paderewski, Venizélos, and Brătianu) also be sought.[26] As Lloyd George reported to the Council of Four on the following day, Paderewski and Venizélos were firmly in favor of granting this right to Council members only.[27] The issue was debated for the last time on June 16; on this occasion Lloyd George announced that Venizélos was now of the opinion that the right to activate the guarantee mechanism should only be given to the *permanent* members of the Council. (There is no explanation in the protocol of the meeting as to why Venizélos abandoned the position he had adopted ten days earlier.) Wilson also revealed that Beneš shared the same view and suggested that this right be given to members of the Council rather than to every member of the League.

According to the protocol, the participants finally agreed to invest this power only in the permanent members of the Council.[28] But this decision was at variance with the Polish minority protection treaty, signed on June 28, which granted such a right to every member of the Council, and eventually the practice laid down in the Polish minority protection treaty was adopted.

Accepted legal procedure implied that members of the Council had to be advised of incoming petitions, since this was crucial to any one member deciding to give its backing. The Tittoni report solved the problem by recommending that the Secretary-General inform every member of the Council (together with the state concerned) about the petitions sent to the Secretariat. In this way any Council member might activate the guarantee mechanism, if it felt obliged to do so. Moreover, such a procedure would enable the state implicated in the matter to inform the Council of its position.

The most momentous result of the Tittoni report's adoption was the fact that from then on the minorities themselves were able to turn to the League in matters concerning the violation of minority rights. And although a petition could only succeed in initiating the League of Nations' guarantee procedure when at least one Council member supported it, the petition system itself proved vital to the protection of minorities, regardless of the fact that only a small proportion of the petitions resulted in a legal action by the League of Nations.

The petitions were meant to be informative; therefore, anybody could submit them: a person, a group of persons, a corporate body or other organization. Petitions had to be judged on their content, not on the individuals or organizations responsible for submitting them.

The possibility of handing in petitions, and the sheer number of the petitions that actually arrived, necessitated regulations to govern the way in which they were to be processed. A number of resolutions aided the handling and processing of the petitions. (These were passed on October 25, 1920; July 27, 1921; September 5, 1923; June 10, 1925; and June 13, 1929.)* When the Council's resolutions were being formulated, the debates and the resolutions of the annual General Assemblies were taken into account to a significant degree.

On the basis of the above resolutions, in the second half of the 1920s a definite procedure was worked out in connection with petitions. A Minorities Section was formed within the Secretariat which, in addition to gathering information, performed the task of classifying the petitions as "receivable" or "non-receivable."[29] For a petition to be "receivable," a number of criteria had to be satisfied; these were listed under five points in a Council's resolution adopted on September 5, 1923 and were as follows:

1. The petition had to keep in view protection of minorities in accordance with the treaties. This meant that however injurious a certain practice or state of affairs was to the minorities, the League of Nations could only deal with it if it violated one or more of the articles of the internationally-guaranteed minority protection treaties;

2. The petition could not be submitted in the form of a request for the severance of political relations between the minority in question and the state of which it was a part (the somewhat ambiguous phrasing of this point referred to the obligation of the racial, religious, and linguistic minorities to cooperate with the majority people as loyal citizens);[30]

---

* For the complete texts of these resolutions, see Appendix 5.

3. The petition could not emanate from an anonymous or unauthenticated source;

4. The petition had to refrain from the use of violent or inflammatory language;

5. The petition had to contain information or refer to facts which had not recently been the subject of a petition already submitted.

If the preliminary study of the Secretariat found the petition "receivable," then the government of the state concerned was informed of this. The government had basically two options. It could accept the petition, in which case it had a limited period to make its comments, after which the Council would receive the petition together with the comments of the government in question. Alternatively, the government could disagree with the Secretariat's verdict and reject the petition as "non-receivable," in which case the petition would be handed to the Chairman of the Council who, after consulting with two other representatives of Council members, would decide the issue of whether the petition was "receivable" or not.

All this was part of the preliminary procedure, in the course of which the petition was either received, or rejected as "non-receivable."

The Council's Minorities Committee grew out of the above practice. Initially, it merely served to decide the admissibility of the petitions, if the state in question disputed the decision of the Secretariat. Later, however, this committee's tasks also included the study of those petitions which had already been admitted to the Council in order to determine whether the petition warranted the initiating of "legal proceedings."

The Minorities Committee of the Council was not a permanent body. It was formed *ad hoc* for the study of specific cases. The Chairman of the Council appointed two members to investigate a given case. Therefore, several "minorities committees" might be conducting parallel investigations during any one session of the Council, and occasionally even between sessions. Having concluded its investigation, a committee would send its report to the members of the Council. This would be published in the League of Nations' official journal, the *Journal Officiel*.

From the above, it should be apparent that, although the

procedure was rather tedious, the measure of progress could not be expressed simply in terms of the number of petitions thus processed.

Professor C. A. Macartney compiled a statistical survey of the four years from 1930 to 1933 based on the official figures published by the League of Nations:[31] the League was sent 419 petitions during this period, nearly half of which (198 petitions) were declared non-receivable.

During the period before 1930, the proportion of petitions meeting the same fate was very similar. Approximately 300 petitions were sent in up to the end of 1929, and nearly half of them were judged non-receivable. It is worth noting the number of petitions with reference to Hungary. Of the thirty-three petitions submitted on behalf of the Hungarian minorities up until the end of 1929, eighteen were received. At the same time, the number of petitions protesting against the conduct of the Hungarian government—most of them provoked by the *numerus clausus* restricting the number of Jews in higher education—was nine.[32]

In the late 1920s and early 1930s, minorities committees were formed to study petitions, judged to be receivable, in an average of thirty to thirty-five cases annually, in other words, approximately half of all receivable cases. The rest of the receivable petitions were handed directly to the members of the Council. Either way, members of the Council had the opportunity to request the initiating of legal action. Since minorities committees were always formed by the Chairman of the Council, it was entirely up to him to decide which receivable petitions should be sent directly to the Council and which should be referred to a minorities committee in order to determine whether the initiating of legal proceedings was justified.

In 1930-31, during the period between two general assemblies, seventy-three petitions were judged to be receivable, and minorities committees were set up in forty-five cases. In addition, twenty-one minorities committees were still working on petitions submitted earlier. This meant that during the above period the Council handled sixty-six petitions at the minorities committee level. In thirty-two cases the committees had concluded their investigations by the time the General Assembly of 1931 was called. In a significant number of cases (fourteen, to be exact), these investigations resulted from petitions which had been submitted before the General Assembly of 1930.[33]

The work of the minorities committees did not constitute a part of "juristic action." It was precisely the task of the minorities committees to determine whether legal action by the Council was justified in a particular case. In practice, eventually the representative of the government implicated in the petition could also take part in a committee's investigations; consequently, attempts could be made to reach a compromise in the matter as early as the preliminary investigations. In the majority of the cases, the minorities committees were able to achieve success at this stage: with only a few exceptions, the work of the minorities committees ended with some type of compromise rather than with the recommendation that the Council start legal proceedings.

Once legal proceedings were initiated in the matter of a petition, it became a dispute of international concern. The handling of such a dispute was regulated by the Covenant of the League of Nations. Instead of quoting the relevant articles, here we only would like to point out that, according to the Covenant, attempts had to be made to reach an agreement. Therefore, the League of Nations and the Council were required to play the role of arbitrator. If it did not prove possible to reach an agreement, then the dispute could be referred to the Permanent Court of International Justice. Again, there were two ways to proceed: it was possible to request either the advisory opinion of the Court or a legal ruling by it. In this way, the Minorities Committee of the Council, which consisted of three Council members (expandable to five if necessary, according to a later resolution), acquired a key role in the decision of the Council on whether to initiate a legal procedure in the matter raised by a petition already found receivable.

The Council began legal proceedings in a relatively small number of cases: only thirteen petitions reached this stage between 1920 and 1931. Nevertheless, the possibility of concluding the dispute by way of a compromise was left open throughout. The Council always aimed at a correct and satisfactory conclusion of the dispute between the minority and the given state; this remained a high priority even after legal proceedings had commenced. In most cases such a settlement was achieved.

In the absence of an acceptable compromise, legal proceedings then involved the Permanent Court of International Justice. The participation of this body was in accordance with the Covenant of the League of Nations, which referred disputes of international concern to it. Even at this juncture, the Court's advisory opinion, rather than its legal ruling, was requested. Since the Court's advisory opinion was always sufficient to produce a compromise between the parties involved, it proved unnecessary to seek the legal ruling of the Permanent Court of International Justice in disputes concerning the minorities.

Article 14 of the Covenant of the League of Nations provided for the establishment of the Permanent Court of International Justice, defining its tasks in international disputes. In its first year, the League of Nations worked out the rules governing this body. In September 1921, justices were elected to the Court by the Council and the General Assembly. The Court began sitting in 1922; it usually held one or two sessions each year.

The first two minority protection cases submitted to the Permanent Court of International Justice concerned the grievances of the German minority living in Poland. One was in connection with the economic disadvantages suffered by the German settlers, the other concerned the question of the German minority's citizenship. On September 10 and 15, 1923, the Court opted in favor of the minorities in both cases (Advisory Opinion No. 6 and No. 7). A compromise then followed, and the Council actively participated in the negotiations which led up to it.[34]

The next three occasions when the Court was asked to give its opinion on minority questions were in 1925, 1928, and 1930—each time in connection with the Greek–Turkish and the Greek–Bulgarian conflicts. In 1931, the Court examined the schooling situation of the German minority in Upper Silesia, and in 1935 it gave its opinion in connection with the minority schools in Albania.

In each case, the Court's advisory opinion was followed by a compromise in favor of the minority concerned. In general, the advisory opinion of the Permanent Court of International Justice, followed by a settlement based on that opinion and satisfying the legitimate claims of the minorities, constituted the highest stage in the League of Nations' guarantee procedure.[35]

It must be emphasized that the solution of the minority problem in East Central Europe was beyond the powers of international minority protection; the effectiveness of the system in general should be judged by its impact. The main value of the League of Nations lay in the beneficial influence it had on the circumstances of the minorities on the one hand, and on the minority policies of states on the other. It is worth recalling the thoughts of a contemporary published in *Magyar Szemle*:

> While it is widely known that the minority protection treaties are far from perfect, and that they come nowhere near to fulfilling their original aims, we would not wish to underestimate the significance of these treaties, since we do not know what the situation would be without them.[36]

The "solution" or the "suitable handling" of the minority problem in East Central Europe at that time could only be found in a relationship between the majority state and the minorities. The institution of international minority protection could help movement towards this, but the creation of such a relationship was really the task of the parties concerned. The assessment of international minority protection is only possible when this is borne in mind. It was the overall permeating effect of international minority protection, rather than the number of the actual cases brought to a conclusion, that mattered. In this respect, despite its deficiencies, the institution of international minority protection did work.

The Congress of European Nationalities

By allowing the petitioning system to operate, the League of Nations encouraged minority groups to form organizations to safeguard minority interests. As early as the first half of the 1920s, the minorities formed various organizations throughout the East Central European belt. These organizations were closely associated with the representation of minority interests, and wherever the opportunity existed, they rallied behind the minorities' parliamentary representatives. They also gave broad support to the cause of minority protection. The organizations of the German minorities became the most important of all such associations; these operated in Czechoslovakia, Poland, Hungary, Romania, Yugoslavia, Italy, Latvia, Estonia, Lithuania, and Denmark.

After the German ones, the most important associations were those of the Jewish national minorities, which had strong organizations in Poland, Lithuania, Latvia, and, later, in Czechoslovakia, Romania, Estonia, and Bulgaria. In Czechoslovakia, the nationality-type Jewish organizations were mostly to be found in the easternmost region, since most Jews of Bohemia considered themselves Germans or Czechs, while Jews living in Slovakia regarded themselves as Hungarians. The situation was similar in the case of Jews living in Romania. In Transylvania, those belonging to the Jewish faith preferred to think of themselves as Hungarians. They identified with the Hungarian minority and were looked upon as Hungarians even by the Romanian government. Therefore, the minority-type Jewish organizations of Romania mostly represented the Jews living in the Regat, Bessarabia, and in those parts of the Bukovina which had been annexed by Romania after World War I.

The Hungarians also formed organized minority groups. Efficiently-operating cultural and political organizations were established by the Hungarians of Czechoslovakia, Romania, and Yugoslavia.

The Ukrainian minority, too, formed organizations, first in Poland and Romania, and later in Czechoslovakia also. The Slovenes boasted strong organizations in Austria, while in Italy they usually joined with the Croatian minority when forming groups. The largest of the Polish minority organizations operated in Germany, and the best-organized Byelorussian groups were to be found in Poland.

In 1925, the organized groups of the national minorities even formed an international body; this was known as the Congress of European Nationalities and held annual assemblies in Geneva, Vienna, or Bern.[37] The idea originated with Dr. Ewald Ammende, the leader of the German minority in Estonia and also a member of the Estonian Parliament. He was greatly encouraged in this enterprize by the success of the nationality movements in Estonia: the Estonian Parliament passed a law in February 1925 granting cultural autonomy to the nationalities. To achieve the same thing in every European state was the main goal set by Ammende for the organization; in this respect he wished to take the internationally-guaranteed minority protection policies established in East Central Europe one step further.

In Ammende's view, the Congress of European Nationalities would be duty bound not only to check the observance of international minority protection treaties, but also to fight for cultural autonomy—precisely in order to facilitate proper handling of the minority issue. Ammende worked out a plan in which he explained why such an organization was necessary, and outlined its program. This plan formed the basis of the negotiations which he conducted with the leaders of the minority groups in various countries. Then, on July 8, 1925, during the congress of the Federation of League of Nations' Societies in Warsaw, preparatory talks were held.*

On August 26, 1925, following the Warsaw discussions, a letter of invitation for a congress to be held in Bern on October 14 was drafted, and sent off to every organized minority group in Europe. In addition to Ammende, three other well-known personalities in the minority movements signed the letter: Dr. J. Wilfan, a member of the Italian Parliament representing Italy's Slovene and Croatian population; Dr. T. Schiemann who represented the German population in the Latvian Parliament; and Géza Szüllö, president of the Hungarian society in the Federation of the League of Nations' Societies of Czechoslovakia.

The letter of invitation revealed that "primarily, the conference will discuss the ways of accomplishing peaceful coexistence, on a civic basis, between the minorities and the majority nation."[38] This objective, as well as the actual work of the Congress (at least until 1933) was clearly in harmony with the minority policies of the League of Nations. In the published program, the invited organizations were asked to study the text of the proposed resolutions and to attend the congress only if they agreed with their content.

---

* In several countries, organizations—called "League of Nations' Societies"— were formed to support the work of the League of Nations. From time to time, these societies held international congresses; one such conference was held in Warsaw.

Accordingly, the proposed resolutions also constituted the theoretical foundations of the Congress and the movement. From this point of view, the proposal for Resolution No. 2 was the most important, and read as follows:

In European states within whose borders more than one ethnic group lives, each such group should be entitled to organize legal bodies on the basis of their various conditions, be they territorial or personal, in order to nourish and promote its culture. In this right to autonomy, the delegates [to the Congress] see a way in which co-operation without friction and based on loyalty can be established between the minority groups of the states concerned, and also one in which links between the peoples of Europe can be promoted.[39]

After thorough preparations, the first congress was held in October 1925. It was attended by the representatives of every organized minority group of the East Central European belt. Thirty-three groups from fourteen countries sent delegates, who represented twelve nationalities.[40] With the exception of the German population of Denmark, every minority group represented at the first congress lived in this zone, and the overwhelming majority of these nationalities were protected under international law; the minority groups of Italy and Germany (not including the minorities of Upper Silesia) were the exceptions to this rule.

The most completely represented national minority was the German: the German minority groups of Czechoslovakia, Poland, Romania, Hungary, Yugoslavia, Italy, Latvia, Estonia, and Denmark all had representatives at the congress. There was only one sizeable German minority (approximately 90,000 persons) outside the countries listed above: this lived in Lithuania, including the *Memelland*. (The following congress was attended by the representatives of the German minority in Memel and its adjacent territory.[41])

The Hungarian minorities were also well represented, since the Hungarian minorities of Czechoslovakia, Romania, and Yugoslavia all sent delegates to the congress. Another well-represented national minority was that of the Poles: Polish delegates came from Germany, Czechoslovakia, Latvia, and Lithuania. (In fact, the Polish delegates attended only the first three congresses, for reasons which will be discussed later.) The Jewish (national) minority groups of Poland, Lithuania, Latvia, and Czechoslovakia all sent delegates. The second congress was also attended by representatives of the Jewish minority living in Bulgaria, and the third by the delegates of Romania's Jews; subsequently, these Jewish minorities were regularly represented.

Delegates of one of the largest minority groups, the Ukrainians of Poland, also attended, although (as we shall see later) in certain years they only attended the congress as observers. Czechoslovakia's Ruthenians were also represented: at the first congress they had a separate delegation, but afterwards joined the other Ukrainian groups. The Ukrainian minority of Romania also sent delegates later. The Slovene minority groups of Austria and Italy played an important part in the work of the congress. The additional nationalities attending the first congress were the Croats, Byelorussians, Russians, Serbs, Danes, Swedes, and Lithuanians. The Catalan minority of Spain and Austria's Czech and Slovak groups attended from the second congress onwards; Romania's Bulgarian minority was represented from 1928 onwards, and Yugoslavia's Bulgarian minority from 1929 onwards. In 1930, the Basque population of Spain and the Greeks of Italy began to send delegates. Therefore, the Congress, which initially brought together only the minorities of the East Central European belt, gradually became a truly European affair.[42]

The Congress of European Nationalities, uniting the organized national minorities of Europe, was burdened with internal frictions from the beginning. These stemmed from the near-impossible task of getting an extremely heterogeneous group of minorities to rally behind a single program. Since the German minorities were instrumental in bringing together the Congress, their specific interests weighed heavily when policy was formulated.

For example, the demand for cultural autonomy modeled on the Estonian example was presented as being in the general interest of all national minorities, but although the majority of the organized national minorities concurred in this view, some departed from it—and in diametrically opposed directions. According to one dissident opinion, cultural autonomy was not enough, and territorial autonomy, or even sovereignty, should be demanded. This view was advocated primarily by the Ukrainian minority in Poland, and it was precisely for this reason that on several occasions their representatives attended congresses only as observers.[43]

The other dissident view was that conditions for assimilation should be guaranteed, and that therefore the goal to aim at was complete equality of civil rights, rather than the segregation represented by cultural autonomy. This latter approach mainly characterized the minorities living in Germany.

The first congress proceeded according to plan, although the two groups of dissident minorities made their voices heard even then. The congress adopted the recommended policies, whereby a minority should aim for cultural autonomy while remaining loyal to the state in which it was living. In accordance with the program, members were elected to a presidium which was to direct the work of the Congress; a committee was also elected to act between conferences and to prepare the forthcoming conference. Thus, the first congress created the conditions for the continuous functioning of an on-going organization; Ammende was elected to the post of general secretary.[44]

The first discordant voice amidst the general unanimity of the first congress came from the Ukrainian, Byelorussian, and Lithuanian minorities living in Poland. Essentially, their statement said that the signatories were not prepared to settle for cultural autonomy; they wanted territorial autonomy, even sovereignty. As the aims of the Congress stopped short of such goals, and in view of the fact that they would still welcome cultural autonomy for their peoples, the signatories of the statement announced that nevertheless they wished to take part in the work of the congress merely as observers.[45]

The organizers' decision not to invite certain national minorities from Germany provoked another controversy. A Polish delegate from Germany expressed his concern over the fact that certain national minorities in Germany, for example, the Lithuanians and the Frisians, had not been asked to attend. Earlier, the same problem had already been raised by the delegate representing Germany's Danish population. In his speech, the Danish delegate hinted at certain fundamental conceptual differences said to exist between the organizers and some of the minorities, differences which could have explained the absences. According to the Danish delegate, the federation of Germany's minorities wished to secure freedom of cultural development for the non-German minorities of the country, without actually demanding cultural autonomy at the institutional level. Obviously, these minorities were further ahead in the process of assimilation, and hoped to develop their cultures unisolated from the majority nation, rather than under conditions of segregation from it.[46]

At the end of the proceedings, a five-member committee was elected for the purpose of preparing the next congress. Consequently, by the time the first congress ended, the permanent body of the movement, the general secretary, and the committee preparing the annual assemblies had all been elected; the committee met several times yearly.

The second congress was called by the committee for August 25, 1926. Like the first congress, it was chaired by Dr. Wilfan; it met in Geneva. Wilfan, who went on to play a major role in the later work of the movement, attempted to preserve the unity of the organization, stressing the following in his opening speech:

> In the working program of our Congress, the guaranteeing of the freedom of cultural development is the first priority.[47]

Accordingly, he did not place too much emphasis on cultural autonomy, but pointed out that freedom of cultural development for the national minorities could not be achieved through a uniform program applicable to every state, since the actual form in which it should be realized, as well as the methods required, could vary considerably from country to country. Therefore, in order to preserve the unity of the conference, Dr. Wilfran hoped to pave the way toward a compromise acceptable to all participants, without abandoning the original program.

Nevertheless, the debate which the Polish and Danish delegates from Germany had started the year before (that is, on whether the Congress's program should concentrate on the minorities' freedom to develop their own culture rather than on the fight for cultural autonomy) again surfaced at the second congress. As the Polish delegate explained, the act of "registering," necessarily involved in the implementation of cu' ural autonomy, could do more harm than good to the national minorities of Germany.[48] And although, in his opening address, the chairman had spoken in general terms about the fight for the freedom of minorities to develop their own culture, the work of the second congress was centered on laying the theoretical foundations for cultural autonomy. Using the Estonian example as a model, the congress drew up its own blueprint for such rights.[49]

The third congress was held in Bern in August 1927. The organizing committee consisted of the same five persons who had been elected at the first conference, and the general secretary, Ammende, played a major part in preparations for it: it was he who co-ordinated the work from an office in Vienna.[50] At this third congress, a major breakthrough was achieved in the theoretical aspects of the minority problem, and for this Arthur Balogh, a professor at the University of Kolozsvár and a prominent member of Transylvania's Hungarian minority, deserves much of the credit.

It was also at the third congress that the first split took place, although at the time it was not a very serious one. Representatives of Germany's Polish and Danish minority groups, unhappy with the response to their earlier objections concerning non-admission to the Congress of the Frisian and Lithuanian minorities in Germany, announced their withdrawal from the organization.[51] The Polish minority groups of some other countries (Latvia, Lithuania, Czechoslovakia) showed their solidarity by not taking part in later congresses.

While expressing trust in the organizers of the Congress, the Jewish delegate Leo Motzkin was also among those who disapproved of the organizers' decision to exclude those national minorities which wished to assimilate. In this way he showed his solidarity with those minority groups choosing the path of assimilation. This seemed natural on Motzkin's part, considering that a significant proportion of European Jews were following the path to assimilation. Therefore, Motzkin equally supported both approaches: he wanted to see the organization represent and protect the interests of the minorities wishing to assimilate, and at the same time demand cultural autonomy for those minorities which required it. This was hardly surprising, since Motzkin represented the nationality-type Jewish organizations of the East Central European belt, which, unlike those Jews opting for assimilation, possessed their own culture (the Yiddish language, etc.) and primarily wanted cultural autonomy.

In the formulation of its policies, the Congress was now shifting noticeably towards the demand for cultural autonomy. But although this resulted in certain minority groups withdrawing their support, the organization continued to represent the overwhelming majority of the national minorities of the East Central European belt right up until 1933. However, following the rift, German dominance further increased, a development which would later have serious implications, as we shall see.

From the point of view of the subject of the present work, the fourth congress, held in 1928, is especially interesting. On this occasion, the minority protection work of the League of Nations was discussed in detail, under the heading "The Situation of the National Minorities and the League of Nations." The general view was that the League of Nations was doing a very poor job of fulfilling its guarantee obligations. Instead of relying on the petitioning system, the League of Nations should, according to its critics at the congress, act on its own initiative to ensure that the minority protection treaties were observed everywhere. One speaker emphasized:

It must be again stressed that the minority treaties constitute an integral part of the peace treaties. It is wrong to think that the tasks of the League of Nations are fulfilled merely by the safeguarding of the present territorial extent of states. It should not be forgotten that states were guaranteed their territory in return for guarantees stating that the League of Nations will protect minorities from all kinds of national oppression on the part of the majority groups. The League of Nations, to which the right of the intervention was transferred by the Great Powers, should therefore demand that these states discharge the duties they took upon themselves in the minority treaties.[52]

The resolution adopted by the congress emphasized that the minority rights guaranteed by the League of Nations could only provide a framework for cooperation between the national minorities and the majority nation of a given country. For this reason, the congress considered it rather unfortunate that the League of Nations was unable even to guarantee satisfactorily those minority rights which had been incorporated in the treaties.[53]

An interesting moment of the fourth congress occurred when the delegation of Poland's Ukrainians announced that it henceforth intended to take part in the work of the congress as a full member, rather than as an observer. The Ukrainian speaker explained that his delegation was still not satisfied with the Congress's program which stopped at cultural autonomy; nevertheless, since even this would advance the cause of the Ukrainian minorities, and since the Ukrainian delegation was convinced that the Congress was genuinely working towards the goal it had set for itself, the Ukrainian delegation felt that its full support was both justified and necessary.[54]

The most important achievement of the fifth congress (1929) was the establishment of a research institute to study the minority problem.[55]

The seventh congress (1931) was notable from Hungary's point of view: it admitted to membership the country's Slovak minority group. Now there were two delegations representing organized national minorities in Hungary: that of the Germans and that of the Slovaks.[56]

During the eighth congress, held in Vienna in 1932, it became apparent that the organization—as a reflection of the current European developments—was heading for a serious crisis. As the introductory report revealed:

...in many countries the tide of chauvinism is rising, and national pride and assertion are giving way to any form of self-expression against all other nationalities.[57]

The speech delivered in praise of the congress's work by a delegate representing the Russian minority of Estonia was hardly prescient. He said that, with chauvinism everywhere on the increase, the congress was almost like a refuge, since here the representatives of the various nations were capable of cooperating at a time when the animosity between nations was, once again, flaring up all over Europe.[58] The events of the 1933 congress shattered such illusions completely.

At the time of its foundation and during the first years of its existence (up until 1932), the Congress of European Nationalities contributed to European efforts to unite Europe. By promoting the minorities' integration with the majority nations and by developing the necessary legal background, the congress worked towards this end.

The difficulties facing the various minorities in the different states were suitably reflected in the history of the first congresses. The events of the early congresses testified to the specific character of each minority's problems and to the impossibility of finding a universally-valid solution. During the years following World War I, however, most of the minority groups attending the Congress of European Nationalities concentrated mainly on adjusting to their new situation and on exercising their minority rights in the given circumstances.

With the year 1933, an utterly new situation developed in European affairs and the direction they were taking; this turn of events greatly affected the minority movements also.

Chapter 5
The Outlook

The Failure of Minority Protection in the 1930s

We have stressed on several occasions that, by itself, the system of international guarantees could not have solved the problem of minority protection, although the united effort to find and work out mutually acceptable measures had a beneficial influence on the handling of minority conflicts. An instant solution to the minority problem could never have been found in so large and ethnically diverse region as East Central Europe, no matter how good a job the drafters of the treaties had done. Here, "the solution" was the continuous and able management of the problem. It should be added, however, that a "uniform" approach to the minority problems was also inadmissible: what constituted improvement for one minority could have been a handicap for another.

Internationally guaranteed minority protection was mostly limited to minimum demands. Although the system encouraged the exploration of additional possibilities, such a development only occurred in countries where the will was present. Still, there were several countries in which even the minimal protection owed to the minorities (in other words, the level provided by the international minority protection treaties) was considered too generous. In the 1920s, however, the latter view still did not prevail, and constructive forces were allowed to operate.

The return of stability during the 1920s also affected the minority movements; throughout that decade they displayed a loyal attitude towards the majority states, as can be seen from the history of the Congress of European Nationalities.

The international protection of minorities, both the written legislation and the actual practice, greatly contributed to the successful bringing of stability to the newly-established political system in East Central Europe, assisting the integration of the minority population into the new state system of the region. The arrangements which served the protection of the minorities in the new states of East Central Europe provided one of the assurances of peace. However, it also worked the other way around: the conditions which allowed the system to operate existed only as long as the forces working for the preservation of peace were in the ascendant.

From 1926, the year Germany joined the League of Nations and acquired a permanent seat on the Council, until 1933, the German government played an important role in the League of Nations' minority protection policies. Gustav Stresemann, who directed German foreign policy, wished to restore Germany's earlier prestige through negotiations and consultation.[1] He firmly supported the large German minorities of East Central Europe in their efforts to preserve their ethnic identity, but without questioning the need for their loyalty towards the states in which they lived. During Stresemann's time as foreign minister, minority protection found in Germany a faithful advocate at the League of Nations and, more importantly, on the Council.

In his book published in 1933 and entitled *International Guarantees of Minority Rights,* Julius Stone, one of the best contemporary Anglo-Saxon experts on the problems of international minority protection, underlined the sharp differences of opinion that existed in assessing the work of the system founded in 1919 and which by then had been in operation for over a decade. Stone summed up his view on the matter as follows:

> There are many, I myself one of their number, who do not believe that the system was foredoomed either to failure or to success, or that the guarantee has been ignored, or that it has always been satisfied. We think that here, as in other vital questions of peace, there will be a long struggle against the anarchical factors in the Family of Nations, and success or failure will be constantly in the balance.[2]

In the present writer's view, Stone's assessment, that of an astute, erudite contemporary who was able to observe the mechanism in operation, still provides a good point of reference today. At the same time, it also indicates that the system did not work in isolation; it had a place and a role in a policy which aimed to preserve peace and to achieve the necessary changes by peaceful means. However, as soon as European politics took a revisionist course, the same mechanism no longer had a role to play in the continent.

After the appointment of Hitler as chancellor, German policies concentrated on preparations for war; Germany left the League of Nations in 1933. The new German government rejected the idea of minority protection as a matter of principle: Nazi ideology, based on the supremacy of one race destined to rule inferior types, could not accommodate the idea of minority protection. According to Nazi ideology, the inferior races needed to be subjugated or even exterminated, certainly not protected. To the German government in Berlin, the eight million Germans scattered throughout East Central Europe represented a tool serving German domination rather than a "minority" in need of guarantees.

The blow dealt by Germany to minority protection was heavy indeed. But other blows rapidly followed, as states bound by minority protection agreements unilaterally renounced their obligations—obligations under which they had chafed from the very outset. These same states showed a concurrent shift towards fascism.

The first government to follow this course was that of Poland. On September 13, 1934, at the General Assembly of the League of Nations, the Polish foreign minister announced that in future his government would not tolerate League of Nations intervention concerning the protection of Poland's national minorities. He also informed the assembled representatives that the basic laws regulating the minorities' rights would continue to apply, regardless. The minister also declared that the Polish government would accept international intervention or supervision in minority issues only if this were extended to all members of the League of Nations.[3]

In his memoirs, published in 1938, Lloyd George remarked that by making this statement Poland had in fact renounced its right to eastern Galicia, which was largely populated by Ukrainians. His reasoning was that in June 1919, when the Supreme Council of the Peace Conference had given Poland permission to annex this territory, it had been on the condition that the autonomy of the region, as well as the political, religious, and personal freedoms of its inhabitants, would be guaranteed by the Allied and Associated Powers. Therefore, by renouncing this guarantee, Poland lost all rights to this region.[4] Perhaps the elderly ex-prime minister was anticipating that within a year or so Poland would lose the same territory following the outbreak of World War II.

Although possibly in a less spectacular fashion, all the other states with international minority protection obligations (with the exception of Czechoslovakia) followed Poland's example.

The international system of minority protection established by the Peace Conference required, as one of the preconditions for its successful operation, peace or, at least, continuing effort on the part of the European powers to preserve peace. Europe's drift towards war ruined the chances for minority protection, and also wrecked the efforts of those minority politicians who advocated loyalty toward the majority states.

The Change in Direction of the Minority Movements during the 1930s

The changes which took place both in European politics and in the international minority protection system exercised an effect on the minority movements, as illustrated by the internal changes in the Congress of European Nationalities.

After the 1932 congress of the organization, the preparations for the 1933 congress began as usual. This was to be held in Bern, on September 16, 1933, the committee decided. Leo Motzkin was a member of this committee, representing the Jewish organizations of Poland, Romania, Latvia, Lithuania, Czechoslovakia, and Bulgaria. (As we have seen, the Jewish organizations formed the second largest group in the Congress, after the group uniting the German minorities.) Motzkin insisted that the new situation in Germany also be debated by the congress, and proposed the draft of a resolution condemning anti-Semitism in Germany.

As stated earlier, the pre-publication of the resolutions expected to be adopted by the congress constituted an organic part of the work of the committee. However, the representative of the

German groups was against such a debate and, therefore, no decision was made in the matter. Having received no answer, Motzkin now wrote to inform the chairman of the committee that the groups represented by him would only participate at the congress.

> ...when you, Mr. Chairman, have, in agreement with the representatives of the German minorities, tabled a draft resolution unequivocally condemning the stripping of Germany's Jews of their rights as inhumane and as a blow to the minority movement, and when those participating in the Congress are allowed free discussion of the situation in Germany.[5]

Since the committee did not reply to Motzkin's letter, the two largest blocs within the movement turned against each other. The rift became final when, during his speech to the congress, Dr. Roth, a German delegate, identified himself with the racist views taken by Nazism:

> The German groups have always been opposed to assimilation. We consider the exclusion from a new people's culture of persons of a different type, and especially of a different race, to be a fundamental right. This has been clear during the course of the last years...[6]

Although they did not participate in the congress, the representatives of the Jewish groups closely followed its developments, since they hoped for an outcome which would enable them to return. On learning about Dr. Roth's speech, they immediately wrote a letter to the congress, describing what forcible "segregation" in Germany really meant. However, since the congress accepted, unopposed, the German representative's speech the Jewish delegates declared their withdrawal from the Congress to be final.

The draft resolution submitted to the congress reflected the views held by the German groups: the "introduction and execution" of the segregative measures were not incompatible with the Congress's principles.[7] Nevertheless, several delegates indicated before the vote that this was no way for the matter to rest. First to speak was Géza Szüllő, who stated: "On behalf of the Hungarian organizations, I would like to announce that we shall abstain." He was joined by the Ukrainian delegate and the representative of the Catalan population of Spain.[8] Such opposition could not be taken lightly; it was obvious that German domination of the congress would become even more pronounced now that the Jewish groups had withdrawn, despite the fact that the Hungarian and the Ukrainian organizations together represented a much larger population than did the German groups. The chairman of the congress, who, incidentally, supported the German position, anticipated the danger of another split and immediately called for an adjournment.

The problem was not, of course, caused by the fact that the leaders of the German minorities wanted to preserve the national character of their own populations and that they hoped to achieve this by insisting on cultural autonomy. In this regard, the congress supported them. Rather, the danger lay in the fact that the German delegates did not recognize the right of a minority to follow the path of assimilation, or worse still, they approved of forcible segregation in order to prevent this.

In order to prevent the split, a compromise was reached during the adjournment. According to this, the groups which earlier threatened to abstain would vote for the proposal, with the proviso that they could add a declaration of their own wording and that the resulting resolution would only be read as a whole. In the meantime, the leaders of the Hungarian and Ukrainian minorities were joined by the delegates of Estonia's Russian and Polish minorities and by the representatives of Poland's Lithuanians. The declaration read as follows:

The wave of expressedly anti-Semitic measures which is now manifesting itself in a number of countries is contrary to human rights.[9]

Although the resolution reflected well on the courage of certain minorities to stick to their principles, as well as to show their solidarity with a minority who had come under attack, it was not enough to save the Congress. German influence in the Congress subsequently increased, and the original aims of the organization were abandoned.

Together with Arthur Balogh, Elemér Jakabffy, a delegate ever since the first congress, represented the Hungarian minority in Romania. Long before the events described above, Jakabffy had realized that German domination might wreck the entire movement, although initially it was mainly the Slavic groups which called attention to the overpowering nature of the German influence. "Under the circumstances, it is up to the Hungarians and the Jews to mediate, prudently and with great diplomatic skills, in order that the right balance be kept in the movement," wrote Jakabffy in the journal *Magyar Szemle* in 1927.[10]

In 1933, German supremacy at the congress was narrowly averted by the initiative of the Hungarian delegates. After 1933, however, there was no way to counter German domination within the movement. The aims of those leading the Germany minority movements more and more fell in with the ambitions of the politicians in Berlin. The protection of minority rights ceased to be the issue at the heart of the movement; it was replaced by service to Germany in its renewed efforts for hegemony in Europe.

The change of direction in German politics, as shown in the policies of the German minority movements, also seriously affected the Hungarian minority movements. Previously, the delegates of the Hungarian and German minorities had often coordinated their actions. As a result of the German minorities' embarkation on a separate political course, the Hungarian minorities in Czechoslovakia, Romania, and Yugoslavia became increasingly isolated. The new direction of the German minority movement "... shows even less solidarity with the Hungarians than did the bourgeois régime which preceded it," wrote *Magyar Szemle* in 1935.[11]

This new direction also produced its own scientific nonsense. In the words of the excellent linguist Lajos Tamás, the "scholarly fable of the early Germanic origins of Transylvania" was revived, as was the theory of Daco-Romanian continuity. "It is no use matching an unsupported theory of continuity with another one of the same mould; this will make neither of them more plausible," wrote Lajos Tamás.[12]

Accordingly, it was not only the system of international minority protection which failed after 1933, but also the cooperation established in the 1920s between the various minority movements.

The National Minorities after World War II

We cannot close our discussion without at least touching upon the entirely novel situation which developed after World War II —a situation which opened a new chapter in the national minority issue.

In the East Central European state system which emerged after World War I, more than thirty million people—nearly one-third of the overall population of the region—formed national minorities. This number was reduced to eight to ten million after World War II, or, in other words, approximately 8 percent of the population of the zone. Unfortunately, precise figures are not available; consequently, we are mostly confined to estimates, in the same way that we were when we dealt with the period following World War I.

During the 1920s, Germans comprised the largest national minority in the region. The largest German national minority blocs were found in Czechoslovakia and Poland. After the end of World War II, the number of Germans fell to between roughly 1,000,000 and 1,500,000, as a result of expulsions, flight, and emigration. The departure of Germans from the region was accompanied by changes in their relative distribution: with its approximately 250,000-strong German population, Hungary probably now has the largest German minority in the region.

With a total population of 6,500,000, the second largest national minority in the region during the 1920s was the Jewish. Most of these Jews fell victim to Hitler's "Final Solution," and most of those who survived the Holocaust either emigrated or were assimilated. Therefore, a Jewish national minority (speaking its own language and displaying other national characteristics) now scarcely exists in the region.

The third largest national minority in East Central Europe during the 1920s consisted of Ukrainians, of whom there were more than five million. As a result of the post-1945 redrawing of the western frontiers of the Soviet Union, nearly the entire Ukrainian population found itself inside the Soviet Union. The same held true for the 2.3 million Byelorussians and Russians of the region. When Poland's western border was revised, Germany's Poles, nearly one million people, came under Polish rule.

Since the border alteration introduced in the Dobrudja in 1940 remained in force, the Bulgarian minority of pre-war Romania, nearly 400,000 people, became Bulgarian citizens. Following Yugoslavia's reorganization into a federal state, in the course of which Macedonia became a republic on an equal footing with the others, there was no longer any sense in talking about a Macedonian minority.

Italy's South Slav population, approximately 500,000 people, found itself inside Yugoslavia as a result of changes in the border between the two countries. Accordingly, the Hungarian minority became the largest national minority in the region, with its size remaining roughly the same as before, about three million.[13] In the Balkans, sizeable minorities were formed, not only by Germans but also by Albanians (1–1.5 million) and by Turks (between 500,000 and one million). The Swedes of Finland (some 500,000 people) comprised another large minority.

The Gypsy population, present in nearly every country of the region, must also be mentioned among the sizeable national minorities. There are various estimates of the size of this minority, of which a few million is probably the most realistic.

The above data, although somewhat lacking in accuracy, still reflects the enormous changes which took place in the relative strengths of the majority and minority populations on the one hand (from a 70:30 ratio to a 92:8 ratio), and in the ranking of countries according to size of minority population. In the state system established in East Central Europe after World War II, therefore, the largest national minority population was the Hungarian (approximately three million). This was followed by the German (1–1.5 million), Albanian (1–1.5 million), Turkish (between 500,000 and 1 million), Swedish (500,000) and indeterminate Gypsy population (most likely a few million). A further 1–1.5 million people lived as minorities in the region, but when their number is broken down according to country or to national minority, the resulting figures all remain below 100,000.

When looking at the minority populations as percentages of the total populations in the individual countries, we also find considerable changes. In the 1920s, the countries with the largest minority populations in percentage terms were Poland and Czechoslovakia (31 percent and 35 percent respectively). After World War II, Romania became the country with the largest minority population, not only in percentage terms, but also numerically (14 percent of the country's population, or about 3 million people).[14]

Therefore, after World War II, the situation of the Hungarian minority in Romania and the relationship between Romania and Hungary came to dominate the national minority issue in East Central Europe.

It is important to realize, however, that although there were changes in the national and ethnic composition of East Central Europe as a whole, the national and ethnic composition of the Carpathian Basin, the main stage of Hungarian history, has remained largely the same. This is in spite of the fact that the region's state system has been altered three times in the course of the twentieth century—in 1918–20, in 1938–41 and in 1945–47.

As a result of the changes, the minority issue ceased to be a problem specific to East Central Europe, and came to weigh on all European countries with some force.

Also, the justification for confining international minority protection to the region was now gone. In December 1947, the Human Rights Commission of the United Nations sought the opinion of the Economic and Social Council of the organization on whether the minority protection treaties signed after World War I could still be considered valid and binding. In March 1948, the Council commissioned the United Nations Secretariat to conduct an investigation into the matter. The resulting study, which was completed in 1950, stated that

> ...reviewing the situation as a whole, one is led to conclude that between 1939 and 1947 the circumstances as a whole changed to such an extent that, generally speaking, the [League of Nations] system [of international protection of minorities] should be considered as having ceased to exist.[15]

The East Central European system of international minority protection was replaced by international agreements guaranteeing the human rights of every European citizen. A prominent American researcher of the subject concluded in a book published in 1962 that

...while the principle of international protection of collective minority rights was increasingly losing ground, the idea of international protection of human rights of the individual was attracting increasing attention and sympathy.[16]

This process reached its climax in the Helsinki Accords and in the international agreements built on them. Subsequently, the international conventions concerning the specific rights and interests of national minorities were incorporated in international agreements formulating universal human rights.

The new process eliminated the grounds for the argument, often put forward in the 1920s by the states compelled to protect their minorities, which criticized the system because it had not been made universally binding. According to the new concept and international law, the obligation of the European states to guarantee human rights for every citizen, including the right of individuals to use their mother-tongue, to receive education in their mother-tongue, and to foster their own culture, was regarded as an international duty. However, just as in the 1920s, this international obligation only prescribed the minimum basic rights. It was then up to each state to find and to work out, within that framework or even outside it if necessary, concrete forms and ways which seemed most appropriate for the handling of minority problems in a given country.

Notes

In Hungary, only one attempt has ever been made to make a thorough study of minority protection during the interwar period. The beginnings of minority protection were described by Zoltán Baranyai—Hungary's representative accredited to the League of Nations Secretariat—in 1931 (see "A kisebbségi szerződések létrejötte" [The Drafting of the Minority Protection Treaties], *Magyar Szemle,* September–December 1931, pp. 190–200 and 285–296.) His main source was David Hunter Miller's twenty-two-volume compilation entitled *My Diary at the Conference of Paris* which had been printed privately in the first half of the 1920s. (One of the forty published copies of this valuable and rare edition can be found among the treasures of Budapest's University Library.) At that time, Baranyai was still unable to use the other basic sources. "The subject has not yet been exhausted... In order to achieve that, one would have to read through the entire archive of the Peace Conference..., the time for that has not yet come," he wrote at the end of his study.

The most exhaustive study published on this subject to date *(Die Minderheitenfrage und die Eutstehung der Minderheitenschutzverträge auf der Pariser Friedenskonferenz 1919)* was written in 1960 by Erwin Viefhaus, who was able to utilize the basic sources published in the meantime, most notably the thirteen-volume American publication *Papers Relating to the Foreign Relations of the United States. The Paris Peace Conference 1919,* (Washington 1942–1947). In his study Viefhaus placed emphasis on the drafting of the Polish treaty, and covered the minority protection treaties signed with Hungary's neighbors, particularly Yugoslavia and Romania, in considerably less detail.

Viefhaus has published an exhaustive bibliography dealing with the partial studies.

Chapter 1
The Restructuring of the State System of East Central Europe and of National Minority Relations after World War I

1. David Hunter Miller, *The Drafting of the Covenant,* (New York, 1928), p. 102. For a similar view expressed in post-1918 American historiography, see: Victor S. Mamatey, "Legalizing the Collapse of Austria–Hungary at the Paris Peace Conference." In: *Austrian History Yearbook,* 1967/3.
2. David Lloyd George, *The Truth About the Peace Treaties,* (London, 1938), I, p. 91.

Chapter 2
The Importance of the Minorities Problem in the Plans for Restructuring

1. Oszkár Jászi, *A Monarchia jövője. A dualizmus bukása és a Dunai Egyesült Államok* (The Future of the Monarchy. The Danubian United States and the Collapse of Dualism), (Budapest, 1918). [Reprinted: Budapest, 1988].
2. United States Department of State, *Papers Relating to the Foreign Relations of the United States. The Paris Peace Conference, 1919,* (Washington, 1942–47), XII, p. 236. (Hereafter: *Papers...*)
3. See its reports. In: *Papers...,* I, pp. 218–237; XII, pp. 240–525.
4. H.W.V. Temperley (ed.), *A History of the Peace Conference of Paris,* (London, 1920–24), VI, p. 239.
5. József Eötvös, *Über die Gleichberechtigung der Nationalitäten in Österreich,* (Pest, 1850), p. 19.
6. Geoffrey Bruun and Victor S. Mamatey, *The World in the Twentieth Century,* (Boston, 1962), p. 162.
7. *Papers...,* I, pp. 51–52.
8. *ibid.,* p. 58, p. 68.
9. Quoted in Ervin Viefhaus, *Die Minderheitenfrage und die Entstehung der Minderheitenschutzverträge auf der Pariser Friedenskonferenz 1919,* (Würzburg, 1960).
10. In this part I have relied on the data given by Viefhaus.
11. Viefhaus, *op. cit.,* pp. 71–73.
12. For the map based on the book by V.V. Tilea, see: Béla Köpeczi (ed.), *Erdély története* (A History of Transylvania), (Budapest, 1986), III, p. 1730.
13. See among others: E. Flachbarth, *System des internationalen Minderheitrechtes,* (Budapest, 1937), pp. 1–29; C.A. Macartney, *National States and National Minorities,* (London, 1934), pp. 157–178. The notes of both works are included in later basic works.
14. Flachbarth, *op. cit.,* p. 23; Macartney, *op. cit.,* p. 160.
15. Macartney, *op. cit.,* p. 164.
16. *ibid.,* p. 165.
17. Quoted in Lloyd George, *op. cit.,* I, p. 605.
18. Viefhaus, *op. cit.,* pp. 44–45.
19. For the committee, see: Lloyd George: *op. cit.,* I, pp. 606–608.
20. See: Miller, *My Diary at the Conference of Paris,* (New York, 1924; printed

privately), XX, pp. 281–283. (Hereafter: Miller, *My Diary...*). See also: Lloyd George, *op. cit.,* I, pp. 610–611.
21. Lloyd George, *op. cit.,* I, p. 617.
22. The texts are given in Miller, *My Diary...,* III, pp. 31–84; pp. 85–88.
23. Miller, *My Diary...,* I, p. 63.
24. *ibid.,* pp. 337–341.
25. *ibid.,* p. 342.
26. *ibid.,* p. 347. For the text, see: Miller, *My Diary...,* IV, pp. 354–357.
27. Viefhaus, *op. cit.,* p. 42.
28. Zoltán Baranyai, "A kisebbségi szerződések létrejötte. I.," (The Drafting of the Minority Treaties), *Magyar Szemle,* XIII (September–December 1931), p. 192.
29. See Hungary's Corpus Juris, Law XLIV of 1868.
30. Jászi, *op. cit.,* pp. 110–113.

Chapter 3
The Drafting of the Minority Protection Treaties

1. *Papers...,* VI, p. 20. (The May 24 sitting.)
2. *Papers...,* V, pp. 393–395.
3. Paul Mantoux, *Les Délibérations du Conseil du Quatre (24 mars–28 juin). Notes de l'Officier Interprète Paul Mantoux,* (Paris, 1955), I, pp. 440–441.
4. *Papers...,* V, pp. 439–444.
5. *Papers...,* VI, p. 823.
6. *ibid.,* p. 948.
7. *Papers...,* XI, p. 585 (Colonel House's May 22 summary for President Woodrow Wilson).
8. *ibid.,* p. 586.
9. Miller, *My Diary...,* XIII, p. 32.
10. *ibid.,* pp. 44–46.
11. *ibid.,* pp. 84–85.
12. *Papers...,* V, pp. 678–681; Mantoux, *op. cit.,* II, pp. 92–94.
13. The complete text of the treaty is given in Temperley, *op. cit.,* V, pp. 437–446. For the preamble and first chapter in Hungarian, see: Dénes Halmosy, *Nemzetközi szerződések 1919–1945* (International Treaties, 1919–1945), (Budapest, 1983).
14. *Papers...,* XI, p. 393, p. 479.
15. *Papers...,* V, pp. 816–817.
16. Temperley, *op. cit.,* V, p. 129.
17. Quoted in Shermen David Spector, *Rumania at the Paris Peace Conference. A Study of the Diplomacy of Ioan I.C. Brătianu,* (New York, 1962), p. 137.
18. Miller, *My Diary...,* XIII, pp. 74–75.
19. *ibid.,* pp. 85–86.
20. *ibid.,* pp. 89–90; *Papers...,* VI, p. 88.
21. *Papers...,* VI, p. 84; Miller, *My Diary...,* XIII, pp. 97–98.
22. See his notebook. In: *Papers...,* III, pp. 394–410.
23. Miller, *My Diary...,* XIII, p. 99.
24. *Papers...,* VI, p. 131.

25. Its text is given in Miller, *My Diary...*, XIII, pp. 171–179, and in *Papers...*, VI, pp. 535–540.
26. The minorities committee met on June 19: Miller, *My Diary...*, XIII, pp. 189–193.
27. For the report, see: *Papers...*, VI, pp. 570–573. The debate is on pages 569 to 570. See also: Mantoux, *op. cit.*, II, p. 470.
28. *Papers...*, VI, p. 626.
29. *ibid.*, pp. 723–725.
30. *Papers...*, III, p. 423.
31. Viefhaus, *op. cit.*, p. 212.
32. For the text of the Czechoslovak minority treaty, see: Temperley, *op. cit.*, V, pp. 461–470.
33. *Papers...*, VI, p. 45.
34. For the text, see: Temperley, *op. cit.*, V, pp. 197–198.
35. For the problem, see: Miller, *My Diary...*, XIII., pp. 189–193.
36. *ibid.*, pp. 359–360.
37. *Papers...*, VIII, p. 807.
38. *ibid.*, pp. 30–35.
39. Miller, *My Diary...*, XIII, pp. 450–455.
40. *Papers...*, VIII, p. 807.
41. Temperley, *op. cit.*, V, p. 316.
42. For the text of the declaration, see: Temperley, *op. cit.*, V, pp. 382–383.
43. Miller, *My Diary...*, XIII, pp. 144–145.
44. For the committee's debate and report, see: Miller, *My Diary...*, XIII, pp. 269–288.
45. Viefhaus, *op. cit.*, pp. 51–56.
46. Miller, *My Diary...*, XIII, pp. 381–382, 399.
47. *ibid.*, 436–437.
48. *Papers...*, VII, pp. 567–569.
49. *ibid.*, p. 555.
50. For this, see: Spector, *op. cit.*, p. 170.
51. For this, see the notebook drawn up from the August 20 discussions of the American peace delegation. In: *Papers...*, XI, p. 393.
52. *Papers...*, VIII, p. 59.
53. *ibid.*, p. 79.
54. *ibid.*, p. 110.
55. *ibid.*, p. 113.
56. *ibid.*, p. 118.
57. Spector, *op. cit.*, pp. 187–188.
58. *Papers...*, IX, p. 127.
59. *ibid.*, p. 184.
60. Spector, *op. cit.*, p. 215.
61. Temperley, *op. cit.*, V, p. 149.
62. *Papers...*, IX, p. 539.
63. Temperley, *op. cit.*, V, p. 149.
64. Quoted in Zoltán Baranyai, "A kisebbségi szerződések létrejötte. II." (The

Drafting of the Minority Treaties. Part II), *Magyar Szemle,* XIII (September-December 1931), p. 287.

65. Temperley, *op. cit.,* V, p. 454.
66. Arthur Balogh, *A kisebbségek nemzetközi védelme a kisebbségi szerződések és a békeszerződés alapján* (International Protection of Minorities on the Basis of the Minority Treaties and the Peace Treaty), (Berlin, 1928), p. 36.
67. Spector, *op. cit.,* p. 218; *Papers...,* XI, p. 700.
68. *Papers...,* IX, p. 559.
69. See the text in the official publication of the League of Nations: League of Nations, *Protection of Linguistic, Racial and Religious Minorities by the League of Nations,* C.L. 110. I.B. Min. 1927 I.B. 2, p. 23. (Hereafter: *Protection...*)
70. *A magyar béketárgyalások. Jelentés a magyar békeküldöttség működéséről* (The Hungarian Peace Negotiations. A Report on the Work of the Hungarian Peace Delegation), (Budapest, 1920–24), p. xvi. (Hereafter: *A magyar béketárgyalások...*). See also: *Papers...,* IX, p. 405.
71. On this, see: Miller, *My Diary...,* XIII, pp. 364, 374–377.
72. *A magyar béketárgyalások...* II, p. 78.
73. Articles 51, 57 and 60.
74. *A magyar béketárgyalások...,* II, p. 78.
75. *ibid.,* p. 489.
76. *loc. cit.*
77. *A magyar béketárgyalások...,* II, p. 488.

Chapter 4
The International Guarantees in Practice

1. See the publication of the League of Nations Secretariat: *Der Völkerbund. Seine Verfassung und Organisation,* (Genf, 1923), p. 5.
2. *ibid.,* p. 53.
3. For the Covenant of the League of Nations (in Hungarian), see: Halmosy, *op. cit.,* pp. 40–52.
4. League of Nations, *The Record of the First Assembly Plenary Meetings,* (Geneva, 1920), p. 102. (Hereafter: *Record of the First Assembly...*)
5. *Protection...,* pp. 9, 12, 24, 30, 44, 53, 63, 94, 98.
6. League of Nations, *Treaty Series. Publication of Treaties and International Agreements Registered with the Secretariat of the League of Nations.*
7. See the publication of the League of Nations Secretariat: *Der Völkerbund und der Schütz der Minderheiten,* (Genf, 1923). (Hereafter: *Der Völkerbund...*)
8. Record of the First Assembly..., p. 568–569.
9. League of Nations, *A Survey, a Directory and a Who's Who of the League,* (London, 1927), p. 20.
10. Flachbarth, *op. cit.,* p. 447.
11. *ibid.,* pp. 445–446.
12. *Protection...,* p. 17.
13. For the text, see: *Protection...,* pp. 4–5.
14. Macartney, *op. cit.,* p. 260.

15. For the text, see: *Protection...*, p. 65–67.
16. *Der Völkerbund...*, p. 21.
17. For the text of the Declarations, see: *Protection...*, pp. 14–15, 32, 34–36.
18. *ibid.*, p. 38.
19. Flachbarth, *op. cit.*, pp. 331–332.
20. *ibid.*, pp. 336–338.
21. The antecedents of the Estonian autonomy law are ably collected together in Béla Beller, "Az európai nemzetiségi kongresszusok és Magyarország a kisebbségvédelem rendszerében (1925–1929)" (European Nationality Congresses and Hungary in the System of Minority Protection, 1925–1929), *Századok*, 1981, pp. 1006ff.
22. Halmosy, *op. cit.*, p. 40.
23. For a comprehensive description of the guarantee procedure, one of the best works of the time is Julius Stone, *International Guarantees of Minority Rights*, (Oxford–London, 1932).
24. Stone, *op. cit.*, p. 197.
25. Macartney, *op. cit.*, p. 311.
26. *Papers...*, VI, pp. 221–222.
27. *ibid.*, p. 241.
28. *ibid.*, p. 514.
29. For the working out of this section, see Stone, *op. cit.*, pp. 46 ff.
30. Quoted in Zoltán Baranyai, *A kisebbségi jogok védelmének kézikönyve* (Miority Rights Protection: A Handbook), (Budapest, 1925), p. 149.
31. Macartney, *op. cit.*, p. 338.
32. Elemér Radisics, "Egységet a kisebbségvédelemben!" (A United Front on Minority Protection!), *Magyar Szemle*, IX (1930), p. 37.
33. Macartney, *op. cit.*, p. 338.
34. H. Aufricht, *Guide to League of Nations Publications. A Bibliographical Survey of the Work of the League, 1920–1947*, (New York, 1951), p. 190.
35. *loc. cit.*
36. László Ottlik, "A kisebbségi kérdés tegnap és ma" (The Minority Question Yesterday and Today), *Magyar Szemle*, XXVII (May–August 1936), p. 106.
37. *Sitzungsbericht der ersten Konferenz der organisierten nationalen Gruppen in den Staaten Europas im Jahre 1925 zu Genf*, (Genf, n.d), p. 6.
38. *loc. cit.* The theme has been dealt with by Béla Beller (among other Hungarian writers) in his above-mentioned study. In this, he makes use of documents available in the archives of the Hungarian foreign ministry. He delves little into the yearly *Sitzungsberichts* published on the congresses on which the present work is based.
39. *Sitzungsbericht der ersten Konferenz der organisierten nationalen Gruppen in der Staaten Europas im Jahre 1925 zu Genf*, (Genf, n.d.), p. 6.
40. *ibid.*, p. 12.
41. *Sitzbericht der Zweiten Europäischen Nationalitäten Kongress*, (Genf, 1926), p. 6.
42. The introduction of the *Sitzbericht* published every year listed the participants.
43. *Sitzungsbericht*, 1926, p. 7; *Sitzungsbericht*, 1927, p. 8.
44. *Sitzungsbericht*, 1925, pp. 12–13, 71.
45. *ibid.*, pp. 21–23.

46. *ibid.,* pp. 31, 43, 55.
47. *Sitzungsbericht,* 1926, pp. 8, 15.
48. *ibid.,* pp. 66–67, 74.
49. *ibid.,* pp. 155–157.
50. *Sitzungsbericht,* 1927, p. 9.
51. *ibid.,* pp. 123, 125.
52. *Sitzungsbericht,* 1928, p. 52.
53. *ibid.,* pp. 81–82, 162–163.
54. *ibid.,* p. 63.
55. *Sitzungsbericht,* 1929, pp. 147–161.
56. *Sitzungsbericht,* 1931, pp. 146.
57. *Sitzungsbericht,* 1932, pp. 7.
58. *ibid.,* p. 24.

Chapter 5
The Outlook

1. On this, see: Bernhard-Jurgen Wendt, *Grossdeutschland,* (1987), p. 50.
2. Stone, *op. cit.,* p. vii.
3. Janowsky, *op. cit.,* p. 127; Also: *Official Journal, Special Supplement,* No. 125, pp. 42–43.
4. Lloyd George, *op. cit.,* II, p. 1395.
5. *Sitzungsbericht,* 1933, p. 2.
6. *ibid.,* p. 26.
7. *ibid.,* p. 69.
8. *ibid.,* p. 70.
9. *loc. cit.*
10. Elemér Jakabffy, "A szervezett nemzetkisebbségek genfi kongresszusai és a magyar kisebbségek" (The Hungarian Minorities and the Geneva Congresses of the Organized National Minorities), *Magyar Szemle,* I (September–December 1927), p. 176.
11. Gyula Zathureczky, "A magyar kisebbség Romániában" (The Hungarian Minority in Romania), *Magyar Szemle,* XXIV (May–August 1935), p. 386; see also: Endre Moravek, "A német kisebbségek az utódállamokban" (The German Minorities in the Successor States), *Magyar Szemle,* XXVII (May–August 1936), pp. 15–26.
12. Lajos Tamás, "Az ősgermán Erdély tudományos meséje" (The Scholarly Fable of Early Germanic Transylvania), *Magyar Szemle,* XXVII (May–August 1936), pp. 281, 284.
13. For data on the Hungarian minorities, see: Zoltán Dávid, "A magyar nemzetiségi statisztika múltja és jelene" (Statistics Past and Present on the Hungarian National Minorities), *Valóság,* 1980/8. Also: Kázmér Nagy, *Elvesztett alkotmány* (A Lost Constitution), (München, 1974), p. 81.
14. 1978 data. *Zsebatlasz* (Pocket Atlas). p. 95.
15. J.B. Schechtman, *Postwar Population Transfers in Europe, 1945–1955,* (Philadelphia, 1962), p. 18.
16. *ibid.,* p. 19.

Appendix 1

President Wilson's Speech at the Plenary Session
of the Peace Conference, May 31, 1919*

'Mr. President, I should be very sorry to see this meeting adjourn with permanent impressions such as it is possible have been created by some of the remarks that our friends have made. I should be very sorry to have the impression lodged in your minds that the great powers desire to assume or play any arbitrary rôle in these great matters, or assume, because of any pride of authority, to exercise any undue influence in these matters, and therefore I want to call your attention to one aspect of these questions which has not been dwelt upon.

We are trying to make a peaceful settlement, that is to say, to eliminate those elements of disturbance, so far as possible, which may interfere with the peace of the world, and we are trying to make an equitable distribution of territories according to the race, the ethnographical character of the people inhabiting those territories.

And back of that lies this fundamentally important fact that when the decisions are made, the allied and associated powers guarantee to maintain them. It is perfectly evident, upon a moment's reflection, that the chief burden of their maintenance will fall upon the greater powers. The chief burden of the war fell upon the greater powers, and if it had not been for their action, their military action, we would not be here to settle these questions. And, therefore, we must not close our eyes to the fact that in the last analysis the military and naval strength of the great powers will be the final guarantee of the peace of the world.

In those circumstances is it unreasonable and unjust that not as dictators but as friends the great powers should say to their associates: "We cannot afford to guarantee territorial settlements which we do not believe to be right, and we cannot agree to leave elements of disturbance unremoved, which we believe will disturb the peace of the world"?

---

* Quoted in: H.W.V. Temperly, (ed.), *A History of the Peace Conference of Paris,* (London 1920–24), V, pp. 130–132.

Take the rights of minorities. Nothing, I venture to say, is more likely to disturb the peace of the world than the treatment which might in certain circumstances be meted out to minorities. And, therefore, if the great powers are to guarantee the peace of the world in any sense is it unjust that they should be satisfied that the proper and necessary guarantee has been given?

I beg our friends from Rumania and from Serbia to remember that while Rumania and Serbia are ancient sovereignties the settlements of this conference are adding greatly to their territories. You cannot in one part of our transdactions treat Serbia alone and in all of the other parts treat the kingdom of the Serbs, the Croats and the Slovenes as a different entity, for they are seeking the recognition of this conference as a single entity, and if this conference is going to recognize these various powers as new sovereignties within definite territories, the chief guarantors are entitled to be satisfied that the territorial settlements are of a character to be permanent, and that the guarantees given are of a character to insure the peace of the world.

It is not, therefore, the interventions of those who would interfere, but the action of those who would help. I beg that our friends will take that view of it, because I see no escape from that view of it.

How can a power like the United States, for example—for I can speak for no other—after signing this treaty, if it contains elements which they do not believe will be permanent, go three thousand miles away across the sea and report to its people that it has made a settlement of the peace of the world? It cannot do so. And yet there underlies all of these transactions the expectation on the part, for example, of Rumania, and of Czecho-Slovakia, and of Serbia, that if any covenants of this settlement are not observed, the United States will send her armies and her navies to see that they are observed.

In those circumstances, is it unreasonable that the United States should insist upon being satisfied that the settlements are correct? Observe, Mr. Bratiano—and I speak of his suggestions with the utmost respect—suggested that we could not, so to say, invade the sovereignty of Rumania, an ancient sovereignty, and make certain prescriptions with regard to the rights of minorities. But I beg him to observe that he is overlooking the fact that he is asking the sanction of the allied and associated powers for great additions of territory which come to Rumania by the common victory of arms, and that, therefore, we are entitled to say: "If we agree to these additions of territory we have the right to insist upon certain guaranties of peace."

I beg my friend Mr. Kramar and my friend Mr. Trumbic and my friend Mr. Bratiano to believe that if we should feel that it is best to leave the words which they have wished to omit in the treaty, it is not because we want to insist upon unreasonable conditions, but that we want the treaty to accord to us the right of judgment as to whether those are things which we can afford to guarantee.

Therefore, the impressions with which we should disperse ought to be these, that we are all friends—of course that goes without saying—but that we must all be associates in a common effort, and there can be no frank and earnest association in the common effort unless there is a common agreement as to what the rights and settlements are.

Now if the agreement is a separate agreement among groups of us, that does not meet the object. If you should adopt the language suggested by the Czechoslovakian delegation and the Serbian delegation—the Jugoslovak [?] delegation—that it should be left to negotiations between the principal allied and associated powers and their several delegates, that would mean that after this whole conference is adjourned, groups of them would determine what is to be the basis of the peace of the world. It seems to me that that would be a most dangerous idea to entertain, and, therefore, I beg that we may part with a sense, not of interference with each other, but of hearty and friendly co-operation upon the only possible basis of guaranty. Where the great force lies there must be the sanction of peace.

I sometimes wish, in hearing an argument like this, that I were the representative of a small power, so that what I said might be robbed of any mistaken significance, but I think you will agree with me that the United States has never shown any temper of aggression anywhere, and it lies in the heart of the people of the United States, as I am sure it lies in the hearts of the peoples of the other great powers, to form a common partnership of right, and to do service to our associates, and no kind of dis-service.'

Appendix 2

Letter Addressed to Ignacy Paderewski, Prime Minister of Poland, by the President of the Peace Conference, Transmitting to Him the Treaty to be Signed by Poland Concerning the Protection of Minorities*

SIR, *Paris, June 24, 1919.*

On behalf of the Supreme Council of the Principal Allied and Associated Powers, I have the honour to communicate to you herewith in its final form the text of the Treaty which, in accordance with Article 93 of the Treaty of Peace with Germany, Poland will be asked to sign on the occasion of the confirmation of her recognition as an independent State and of the transference to her of the territories included in the former German Empire which are assigned to her by the said Treaty. The principal provisions were communicated to the Polish Delegation in Paris in May last, and were subsequently communicated direct to the Polish Government through the French Minister at Warsaw. The Council have since had the advantage of the suggestions which you were good enough to convey to them in your memorandum of the 16th June, and as the result of a study of these suggestions modifications have been introduced in the text of the Treaty. The Council believe that it will be found that by these modifications the principal points to which attention was drawn in your memorandum have, in so far as they relate to specific provisions of the Treaty, been adequately covered.

In formally communicating to you the final decision of the Principal Allied and Associated Powers in this matter, I should desire to take this opportunity of explaining in a more formal manner than has hitherto been done the considerations by which the Principal Allied and Associated Powers have been guided in dealing with the question.

1. In the first place, I would point out that this Treaty does not constitute any fresh departure. It has for long been the established procedure of the public law of Europe that when a State is

---

* Quoted in: H.W.V. Temperley, (ed.): *A History of the Peace Conference of Paris,* (London, 1920–24), V, pp. 432–437.

created, or even when large accessions of territory are made to an established State, the joint and formal recognition by the Great Powers should be accompanied by the requirement that such State should, in the form of a binding international convention, undertake to comply with certain principles of government. This principle, for which there are numerous other precedents, received the most explicit sanction when, at the last great assembly of European Powers—the Congress of Berlin—the sovereignty and independence of Serbia, Montenegro, and Roumania were recognised. It is desirable to recall the words used on this occasion by the British, French, Italian, and German Plenipotentiaries, as recorded in the Protocol of the 28th June, 1878:

'Lord Salisbury recognises the independence of Serbia, but is of opinion that it would be desirable to stipulate in the Principality the great principle of religious liberty.

*

'Mr. Waddington believes that it is important to take advantage of this solemn opportunity to cause the principles of religious liberty to be affirmed by the representatives of Europe. His Excellency adds that Serbia, who claims to enter the European family on the same basis as other States, must previously recognise the principles which are the basis of social organisation in all States of Europe and accept them as a necessary condition of the favour which she asks for.

*

'Prince Bismarck, associating himself with the French proposal, declares that the assent of Germany is always assured to any motion favourable to religious liberty.

'Count de Launay says that, in the name of Italy, he desires to adhere to the principle of religious liberty, which forms one of the essential bases of the institutions in his country, and that he associates himself with the declarations made on this subject by Germany, France, and Great Britain.

'Count Andrassy expresses himself to the same effect, and the Ottoman Plenipotentiaries raise no objection.

'Prince Bismarck, after having summed up the results of the

vote, declares that Germany admits the independence of Serbia, but on condition that religious liberty will be recognised in the Principality. His Serene Highness adds that the Drafting Committee, when they formulate this decision, will affirm the connection established by the Conference between the proclamation of Serbian independence and the recognition of religious liberty.'

2. The Principal Allied and Associated Powers are of opinion that they would be false to the responsibility which rests upon them if on this occasion they departed from what has become an established tradition. In this connection I must also recall to your consideration the fact that it is to the endeavours and sacrifices of the Powers in whose name I am addressing you that the Polish nation owes the recovery of its independence. It is by their decision that Polish sovereignty is being re-established over the territories in question and that the inhabitants of these territories are being incorporated in the Polish nation. It is on the support which the resources of these Powers will afford to the League of Nations that for the future Poland will to a large extent depend for the secure possession of these territories. There rests, therefore, upon these Powers an obligation, which they cannot evade, to secure in the most permanent and solemn form guarantees for certain essential rights which will afford to the inhabitants the necessary protection whatever changes may take place in the internal constitution of the Polish State.

It is in accordance with this obligation that Clause 93 was inserted in the Treaty of Peace with Germany. This clause relates only to Poland, but a similar clause applies the same principles to Czecho-Slovakia, and other clauses have been inserted in the Treaty of Peace with Austria and will be inserted in those with Hungary and with Bulgaria, under which similar obligations will be undertaken by other States, which under those Treaties receive large accessions of territory.

The consideration of these facts will be sufficient to show that by the requirement addressed to Poland at the time when it receives in the most solemn manner the joint recognition of the re-establishment of its sovereignty and independence and when large accessions of territory are being assigned to it, no doubt is thrown upon the sincerity of the desire of the Polish Government and the Polish nation to maintain the general principles of justice and liberty. Any such doubt would be far from the intention of the Principal Allied and Associated Powers.

3. It is indeed true that the new Treaty differs in form from earlier Conventions dealing with similar matters. The change of form is a necessary consequence and an essential part of the new system of international relations which is now being built up by the establishment of the League of Nations. Under the older system the guarantee for the execution of similar provisions was vested in the Great Powers. Experience has shown that this was in practice ineffective, and it was also open to the criticism that it might give to the Great Powers, either individually or in combination, a right to interfere in the internal constitution of the States affected which could be used for political purposes. Under the new system the guarantee is entrusted to the League of Nations. The clauses dealing with this guarantee have been carefully drafted so as to make it clear that Poland will not be in any way under the tutelage of those Powers who are signatories to the Treaty.

I should desire, moreover, to point out to you that provision has been inserted in the Treaty by which disputes arising out of its provisions may be brought before the Court of the League of Nations. In this way differences which might arise will be removed from the political sphere and placed in the hands of a judicial court, and it is hoped that thereby an impartial decision will be facilitated, while at the same time any danger of political interference by the Powers in the internal affairs of Poland will be avoided.

4. The particular provisions to which Poland and the other States will be asked to adhere differ to some extent from those which were imposed on the new States at the Congress of Berlin. But the obligations imposed upon new States seeking recognition have at all times varied with the particular circumstances. The Kingdom of the United Netherlands in 1814 formally undertook precise obligations with regard to the Belgian provinces at that time annexed to the kingdom which formed an important restriction on the unlimited exercise of its sovereigtnty. It was determined at the establishment of the Kingdom of Greece that the

Government of that State should take a particular form, viz., it should be both monarchical and constitutional; when Thessaly was annexed to Greece, it was stipulated that the lives, property, honour, religion and customs of those of the inhabitants of the localities ceded to Greece who remained under the Hellenic administration should be scrupulously respected, and that they should enjoy exactly the same civil and political rights as Hellenic subjects of origin. In addition, very precise stipulations were inserted safeguarding the interests of the Mohammedan population of these territories.

The situation with which the Powers have now to deal is new, and experience has shown that new provisions are necessary. The territories now being transferred both to Poland and to other States inevitably include a large population speaking languages and belonging to races different from that of the people with whom they will be incorporated. Unfortunately, the races have been estranged by long years of bitter hostility. It is believed that these populations will be more easily reconciled to their new position if they know that from the very beginning they have assured protection and adequate guarantees against any danger of unjust treatment or oppression. The very knowledge that these guarantees exist will, it is hoped, materially help the reconciliation which all desire, and will indeed do much to prevent the necessity of its enforcement.

5. To turn to the individual clauses of the present Treaty, Article 2 guarantees to all inhabitants those elementary rights, which are, as a matter of fact, secured in every civilised State. Clauses 3 to 6 are designed to insure that all the genuine residents in the territories now transferred to Polish sovereignty shall in fact be assured of the full privileges of citizenship. Articles 7 and 8, which are in accordance with precedent, provide against any discrimination against those Polish citizens who by their religion, their language, or their race, differ from the large mass of the Polish population. It is understood that, far from raising any objection to the matter of these articles, the Polish Government have already, of their own accord, declared their firm intention of basing their institutions on the cardinal principles enunciated therein.

The following articles are of rather a different nature in that they provide more special privileges to certain groups of these minorities. In the final revision of these latter articles, the Powers have been impressed by the suggestions made in your memorandum of the 16th June, and the articles have in consequence been subjected to some material modifications. In the final text of the Treaty it has been made clear that the special privileges accorded in Article 9 are extended to Polish citizens of German speech only in such parts of Poland as are, by the Treaty with Germany, transferred from Germany to Poland. Germans in other parts of Poland will be unable under this article to claim to avail themselves of these privileges. They will therefore in this matter be dependent solely on the generosity of the Polish Government, and will in fact be in the same position as German citizens of Polish speech in Germany.

6. Clauses 10 and 12 deal specifically with the Jewish citizens of Poland. The information at the disposal of the Principal Allied and Associated Powers as to the existing relations between the Jews and the other Polish citizens has led them to the conclusion that, in view of the historical development of the Jewish question and the great animosity aroused by it, special protection is necessary for the Jews in Poland. These clauses have been limited to the minimum which seems necessary under the circumstances of the present day, viz. the maintenance of Jewish schools and the protection of the Jews in the religious observance of their Sabbath. It is believed that these stipulations will not create any obstacle to the political unity of Poland. They do not constitute any recognition of the Jews as a separate political community within the Polish State. The educational provisions contain nothing beyond what is in fact provided in the educational institutions of many highly organized modern States. There is nothing inconsistent with the sovereignty of the State in recognising and supporting schools in which children shall be brought up in the religious influences to which they are accustomed in their home. Ample safeguards against any use of non-Polish languages to encourage a spirit of national separation have been provided in the express acknowledgment that the provisions of this Treaty do not prevent the Polish State from making the Polish language obligatory in all its schools and educational institutions.

7. The economic clauses contained in Chapter II of the Treaty

have been drafted with the view of facilitating the establishment of equitable commercial relations between independent Poland and the other Allied and Associated Powers. They include provisions for reciprocal diplomatic and consular representation, for freedom of transit, and for the adhesion of the Polish Government to certain international conventions.

In these clauses the Principal Allied and Associated Powers have not been actuated by any desire to secure for themselves special commercial advantages. It will be observed that the rights accorded to them by these clauses are extended equally to all States who are members of the League of Nations. Some of the provisions are of a transitional character, and have been introduced only with the necessary object of bridging over the short interval which must elapse before general regulations can be established by Poland herself or by commercial treaties or general conventions approved by the League of Nations.

In conclusion, I am to express to you on behalf of the Allied and Associated Powers the very sincere satisfaction which they feel at the re-establishment of Poland as an independent State. They cordially welcome the Polish nation on its re-entry into the family of nations. They recall the great services which the ancient Kingdom of Poland rendered to Europe both in public affairs and by its contributions to the progress of mankind which is the common work of all civilized nations. They believe that the voice of Poland will add to the wisdom of their common deliberations in the cause of peace and harmony, that its influence will be used to further the spirit of liberty and justice, both in internal and external affairs, and that thereby it will help in the work of reconciliation between the nations which, with the conclusion of Peace, will be the common task of humanity.

The Treaty by which Poland solemnly declares before the world her determination to maintain the principles of justice, liberty, and toleration, which were the guiding spirit of the ancient Kingdom of Poland, and also receives in its most explicit and binding form the confirmation of her restoration to the family of independent nations, will be signed by Poland and by the Principal Allied and Associated Powers on the occasion of, and at the same time as, the signature of the Treaty of Peace with Germany.

I have, & c. CLEMENCEAU

Appendix 3

The Treaty Between the Principal Allied and Associated Powers and Romania Concerning Minority Protection*

(Rubric and Chapter1 Only)
Signed at Paris, December 9, 1919.
THE UNITED STATES OF AMERICA, THE BRITISH EMPIRE, FRANCE, ITALY, AND JAPAN,
The Principal Allied and Associated Powers,

on the one hand;

And ROUMANIA,

on the other hand;

Whereas under Treaties to which the Principal Allied and Associated Powers are parties large accessions of territory are being and will be made to the Kingdom of Roumania, and

Whereas Roumania desires of her own free will to give full guarantees of liberty and justice to all inhabitants both of the old Kingdom of Roumania and of the territory added thereto, to whatever race, language or religion they may belong,

Have, after examining the question together, agreed to conclude the present Treaty, and for this purpose have appointed as their Plenipotentiaries, the following, reserving the right of substituting others to sign the Treaty:
THE PRESIDENT OF THE UNITED STATES OF AMERICA:

The Honourable Frank Lyon *Polk,* Under-Secretary of State;

The Honourable Henry *White,* formerly Ambassador Extraordinary and Plenipotentiary of the United States at Rome and Paris;

General Tasker H. *Bliss,* Military Representative of the United States on the Supreme War Council;

---

* Quoted in: League of Nations. *Protection of Linguistic, Racial and Religious Minorities by the League of Nations,* I. B. Minorités 1927. I. B. 2 (C.L. 110. 1927. I), (Geneva, 1927), pp. 51–54.

HIS MAJESTY THE KING OF THE UNITED KINGDOM OF GREAT BRITAIN AND IRELAND AND OF THE BRITISH DOMINIONS BEYOND THE SEAS, EMPEROR OF INDIA:

Sir Eyre *Crowe*, K.C.B., K.C.M.G., Minister Plenipotentiary, Assistant Under-Secretary of State for Foreign Affairs:
And

for the DOMINION of CANADA:

The Honourable Sir George Halsey *Perley*, K.C.M.G., High Commissioner for Canada in the United Kingdom;

for the COMMONWEALTH of AUSTRALIA:

The Right Honourable Andrew *Fisher*, High Commissioner for Australia in the United Kingdom;

for the DOMINION of NEW ZEALAND:

The Honourable Sir Thomas *Mackenzie*, K.C.M.G., High Commissioner for New Zealand in the United Kingdom;

for the UNION of SOUTH AFRICA:

Mr. Reginald Andrew *Blankenberg*, O.B.E., Acting High Commissioner for the Union of South Africa in the United Kingdom;

for INDIA:

Sir Eyre *Crowe*, K.C.B., K.C.M.G.;

THE PRESIDENT OF THE FRENCH REPUBLIC:

Mr. Georges *Clemenceau*, President of the Council, Minister of War;

Mr. Stephen *Pichon*, Minister for Foreign Affairs;

Mr. Louis-Lucien *Klotz*, Minister of Finance;

Mr. André *Tardieu*, Minister for the liberated regions;

Mr. Jules *Cambon*, Ambassador of France;

HIS MAJESTY THE KING OF ITALY:

Sir Giacomo de *Martino*, Envoy Extraordinary and Minister Plenipotentiary;

HIS MAJESTY THE EMPEROR OF JAPAN:

Mr. K. *Matsui*, Ambassador Extraordinary and Plenipotentiary of H.M. the Emperor of Japan at Paris;

HIS MAJESTY THE KING OF ROUMANIA:

General Constantin *Coanda*, Corps Commander, A.D.C. to the King, formerly President of the Council of Ministers;

WHO HAVE AGREED AS FOLLOWS:

CHAPTER I

Article 1.

Roumania undertakes that the stipulations contained in Articles 2 to 8 of this Chapter shall be recognised as fundamental laws, and that no law, regulation or official action shall conflict or interfere with these stipulations, nor shall any law, regulation or official action prevail over them.

Article 2.

Roumania undertakes to assure full and complete protection of life and liberty to all inhabitants of Roumania without distinction of birth, nationality, language, race or religion.

All inhabitants of Roumania shall be entitled to the free exercise, whether public or private, of any creed, religion or belief, whose practices are not inconsistent with public order and public morals.

Article 3.

Subject to the special provisions of the Treaties mentioned below, Roumania admits and declares to be Roumanian nationals *ipso facto* and without the requirement of any formality all persons habitually resident at the date of the coming into force of the present Treaty within the whole territory of Roumania, including the extensions made by the Treaties of Peace with Austria and Hungary, or any other extensions which may hereafter be made, if such persons are not at that date nationals of a foreign state other than Austria or Hungary.

Nevertheless, Austrian and Hungarian nationals who are over eighteen years of age will be entitled under the conditions contained in the said Treaties to opt for any other nationality which may be open to them. Option by a husband will cover his wife and option by parents will cover their children under eighteen years of age.

Persons who have exercised the above right to opt must within the succeeding twelve months transfer their place of residence to the State for which they have opted. They will be entitled to retain their immovable property in Roumanian territory. They may carry with them their movable property of every description. No export duties may be imposed upon them in connection with the removal of such property.

Article 4.

Roumania admits and declares to be Roumanian nationals *ipso facto* and without requirement of any formality persons of Austrian* Hungarian nationality who were born in the territory transferred to Roumania by the Treaties of Peace with Austria and Hungary, or subsequently transferred to her, of parents habitually resident there, even if at the date of the coming into force of the present Treaty they are not themselves habitually resident there.

Nevertheless, within two years after the coming into force of the present Treaty, these persons may make a declaration before the competent Roumanian authorities in the country in which they are resident, stating that they abandon Roumanian nationality, and they will then cease to be considered as Roumanian nationals. In this connection a declaration by a husband will cover his wife, and a declaration by parents will cover their children under eighteen years of age.

Article 5.

Roumania undertakes to put no hindrance in the way of the exercise of the right which the persons concerned have, under the Treaties concluded or to be concluded by the Allied and Associated Powers with Austria or Hungary, to choose whether or not they will acquire Roumanian nationality.

Article 6.

All persons born in Roumanian territory who are not born nationals of another State shall *ipso facto* become Roumanian nationals.

Article 7.

Roumania undertakes to recognise as Roumanian nationals *ipso facto* and without the requirement of any formality Jews inhabiting any Roumanian territory, who do not possess another nationality.

---

* The word "or" is evidently omitted here.

Article 8.

All Roumanian nationals shall be equal before the law and shall enjoy the same civil and political rights without distinction as to race, language or religion.

Differences of religion, creed or confession shall not prejudice any Roumanian national in matters relating to the enjoyment of civil or political rights, as for instance admission to public employments, functions and honours, or the exercise of professions and industries.

No restriction shall be imposed on the free use by any Roumanian national of any language in private intercourse, in commerce, in religion, in the press or in publications of any kind, or at public meetings.

Notwithstanding any establishment by the Roumanian Government of an official language, adequate facilities shall be given to Roumanian nationals of non-Roumanian speech for the use of their language, either orally or in writing, before the courts.

Article 9.

Roumanian nationals who belong to racial, religious or linguistic minorities shall enjoy the same treatment and security in law and in fact as the other Roumanian nationals. In particular they shall have an equal right to establish, manage and control at their own expense charitable, religious and social institutions, schools and other educational establishments, with the right to use their own language and to exercise their religion freely therein.

Article 10.

Roumania will provide in the public educational system in towns and districts in which a considerable proportion of Roumanian nationals of other than Roumanian speech are resident adequate facilities for ensuring that in the primary schools the instruction shall be given to the children of such Roumanian nationals through the medium of their own language. This provision shall not prevent the Roumanian Government from making the teaching of the Roumanian language obligatory in the said schools.

In towns and districts where there is a considerable proportion of Roumanian nationals belonging to racial, religious or linguistic minorities, these minorities shall be assured an equitable share in the enjoyment and application of the sums which may be provided out of public funds under the State, municipal or other budget, for educational, religious or charitable purposes.

Article 11.

Roumania agrees to accord to the communities of the Saxons and Czecklers in Transylvania local autonomy in regard to scholastic and religious matters, subject to the control of the Roumanian State.

Article 12.

Roumania agrees that the stipulations in the foregoing Articles, so far as they affect persons belonging to racial, religious or linguistic minorities, constitute obligations of international concern and shall be placed under the guarantee of the League of Nations. They shall not be modified without the assent of a majority of the Council of the League of Nations. The United States, the British Empire, France, Italy and Japan hereby agree not to withhold their assent from any modification in these Articles which is in due form assented to by a majority of the Council of the League of Nations.

Roumania agrees that any Member of the Council of the League of Nations shall have the right to bring to the attention of the Council any infraction, or any danger of infraction, of any of these obligations, and that the Council may thereupon take such action and give such direction as it may deem proper and effective in the circumstances.

Roumania further agrees that any difference of opinion as to questions of law or fact arising out of these Articles between the Roumanian Government and any one of the Principal Allied and Associated Powers or any other Power, a Member of the League of Nations, shall be held to be a dispute of an international character under Article 14 of the Covenant of the League of Nations. Roumania hereby consents that any such dispute shall, if the other party thereto demands, be referred to the Permanent Court of International Justice. The decision of the Permanent Court shall be final and shall have the same force and effect as an award under Article 13 of the Covenant.

Appendix 4

The Minority Protection Chapter of the Hungarian Peace Treaty*

SECTION VI. — PROTECTION OF MINORITIES**

Article 54.

Hungary undertakes that the stipulations contained in this Section shall be recognised as fundamental laws, and that no law, regulation or official action shall conflict or interfere with these stipulations, nor shall any law, regulation or official action prevail over them.

Article 55.

Hungary undertakes to assure full and complete protection of life and liberty to all inhabitants of Hungary without distinction of birth, nationality, language, race or religion.

All inhabitants of Hungary shall be entitled to the free exercise, whether public or private, of any creed, religion or belief whose practices are not inconsistent with public order or public morals.

Article 56.

Hungary admits and declares to be Hungarian nationals *ipso facto* and without the requirement of any formality all persons possessing at the date of the coming into force of the present Treaty rights of citizenship *(perlinenza)* within Hungarian territory who are not nationals of any other State.

Article 57.

All persons born in Hungarian territory who are not born nationals of another State shall *ipso facto* become Hungarian nationals.

---

* *A magyar béketárgyalások. Jelentés a magyar békeküldöttség működéséről* (The Hungarian Peace Negotiations. A Report on the Work of the Hungarian Peace Delegation), (Budapest, 1920–24), vol. 2.
** Quoted in: League of Nations, *Protection of Linguistic, Racial and Religious Minorities by the League of Nations. Publications de la Société des Nations*, I.B. Minorités 1927. I.B. 2. (C.L. 110. 1927. I.), (Geneva, 1927), pp. 29–30.

Article 58.

All Hungarian nationals shall be equal before the law and shall enjoy the same civil and political rights without distinction as to race, language or religion.

Difference of religion, creed or confession shall not prejudice any Hungarian national in matters relating to the enjoyment of civil or political rights, as for instance admission to public employments, functions and honours, or the exercise of professions and industries.

No restriction shall be imposed on the free use by any Hungarian national of any language in private intercourse, in commerce, in religion, in the press or in publications of any kind, or at public meetings.

Notwithstanding any establishment by the Hungarian Government of an official language, adequate facilities shall be given to Hungarian nationals of non-Magyar speech for the use of their language, either orally or in writing, before the Courts.

Hungarian nationals who belong to racial, religious or linguistic minorities shall enjoy the same treatment and security in law and in fact as the other Hungarian nationals. In particular they shall have an equal right to establish, manage and control at their own expense charitable, religious and social institutions, schools and other educational establishments, with the right to use their own language and to exercise their religion freely therein.

Article 59.

Hungary will provide in the public educational system in towns and districts in which a considerable proportion of Hungarian nationals of other than Magyar speech are resident adequate facilities for ensuring that in the primary schools the instruction shall be given to the children of such Hungarian nationals through the medium of their own language. This provision shall not prevent the Hungarian Government from making the teaching of the Magyar language obligatory in the said schools.

In towns and districts where there is a considerable proportion of Hungarian nationals belonging to racial, religious or linguistic minorities, these minorities shall be assured an equitable share in the enjoyment and application of sums which may be provided out of public funds under the State, municipal or other budgets, for educational, religious or charitable purposes.

Article 60.

Hungary agrees that the stipulations in the foregoing Articles of this Section, so far as they affect persons belonging to racial, religious or linguistic minorities, constitute obligations of international concern and shall be placed under the guarantee of the League of Nations. They shall not be modified without the assent of majority of the Council of the League of Nations. The Allied and Associated Powers represented on the Council severally agree not to withhold their assent from any modification in these Articles which is in due form assented to by a majority of the Council of the League of Nations.

Hungary agrees that any Member of the Council of the League of Nations shall have the right to bring to the attention of the Council any infraction, or any danger of infraction, of any of these obligations, and that the Council may thereupon take such action and give such direction as it may deem proper and effective in the circumstances.

Hungary further agrees that any difference of opinion as to questions of law or fact arising out of these Articles between the Hungarian Government and any one of the Allied and Associated Powers or any other Power, a Member of the Council of the League of Nations, shall be held to be a dispute of an international character under Article 14 of the Covenant of the League of Nations. The Hungarian Government hereby consents that any such dispute shall, if the other party thereto demands, be referred to the Permanent Court of International Justice. The decision of the Permanent Court shall be final and shall have the same force and effect as an award under Article 13 of the Covenant.

Appendix 5

The Resolutions of the Council of the League of Nations Concerning Minority Protection Guarantee Procedures*

1. Report presented by M. Tittoni and adopted by the Council of the League of Nations on October 22nd, 1920

The Council of the League of Nations has thought it advisable to determine the nature and limits of the guarantees with regard to the protection of minorities provided for by the different Treaties.

The stipulations of the Treaties with regard to minorities are generally defined in the following terms:

'The country concerned agrees that the stipulations in the foregoing articles, so far as they affect persons belonging to racial, linguistic or religious minorities, constitute obligations of international concern and shall be placed under the guarantee of the League of Nations.'

The stipulations with regard to minorities declare further that the country concerned 'agrees that any Member of the Council of the League of Nations shall have the right to bring to the attention of the Council any infraction, or any danger of infraction, of any of these obligations, and that the Council may thereupon take such action and give such direction as it may deem proper and effective in the circumstances'.

The countries concerned have further agreed that any difference of opinion as to questions of law or fact arising out of these articles between the Government concerned and any one of the Powers, a Member of the League of Nations, which dispute shall, if the other party thereto demands, be referred to the Permanent Court of International Justice.

Up to the present time, international law has entrusted to the

---

* Quoted in: League of Nations, *Protection of Linguistic, Racial, and Religious Minorities by the League of Nations,* (Geneva, 1931), (C. 8. M. 5. 1931. I.) pp. 7–12.

great Powers the guarantee for the execution of similar provisions. The Treaties of Peace have introduced a new system; they have appealed to the League of Nations.

The Council and the Permanent Court of International Justice are the two organs of the League charged with the practical execution of the guarantee.

It may be advisable at the outset to define clearly the exact meaning of the term 'guarantee of the League of Nations'. It seems clear that this stipulation means, above all, that the provisions for the protection of minorities are inviolable—that is to say, they cannot be modified in the sense of violating in any way rights actually recognized and without the approval of the majority of the Council of the League of Nations. Secondly, this stipulation means that the League must ascertain that the provisions for the protection of minorities are always observed.

The Council must take action in the event of any infraction, or danger of infraction, of any of the obligations with regard to the minorities in question. The Treaties in this respect are quite clear. They indicate the procedure that should be followed.

The right of calling attention to any infraction, or danger of infraction, is reserved to the Members of the Council.

This is, in a way, a right and a duty of the Powers represented on the Council. By this right they are, in fact, asked to take a special interest in the protection of minorities.

Evidently this right does not in any way exclude the right of the minorities themselves, or even of States not represented on the Council, to call the attention of the League of Nations to any infraction, or danger of infraction. But this act must retain the nature of a petition, or a report pure and simple; it cannot have the legal effect of putting the matter before the Council and calling upon it to intervene.

Consequently, when a petition with regard to the question of minorities is addressed to the League of Nations, the Secretary-General should communicate it, without comment, to the Members of the Council for information. This communication does not yet constitute a judicial act of the League or of its organs. The competence of the Council to deal with the question arises only when one of its Members draws its attention to the infraction, or danger of infraction, which is the petition or report.

The State interested, if it is a Member of the League, is informed at the same time as the Council of the subject of the petition. As a matter of fact, the Secretary-General has for some time adopted the procedure of forwarding immediately to all the Members of the League any document forwarded for the information of Members of the Council. This information, which may give the State concerned an opportunity of submitting to the Members of the Council such remarks as it may consider desirable, does not, however, partake of the nature of a request of the League for information with regard to the subject of the petition, nor yet does it imply, with regard to the State concerned, the obligation of furnishing evidence in its defence.

Any cases where, as the result of the petition, the intervention of the League seems to be urgently necessary, the Secretary-General may also adopt the above procedure, but, in view of the urgency of the case, he will forward the petition in question to the Members of the Council as soon as possible (by telegraph if he thinks it advisable).

Each Power represented on the Council may demand that an urgent Council meeting be summoned in accordance with the provisions of the regulations in force.

This precaution will have the object of preventing any sudden act of oppression of minorities.

If the Council approves of the interpretation that I have had the honour to develop, it might adopt the following resolution:

'The Council invites its Members to draw the very special attention of their Governments to the conclusions arrived at in the present report.'

2. *Resolution adopted by the Council on October 25th, 1920*

For a definition of the conditions under which the Council shall exercise the powers granted to it by the Covenant and by various Treaties for the protection of minorities, the Council approved a resolution which will be inserted in its Rules of Procedure:

'With a view to assisting Members of the Council in the exercise of their rights and duties as regards the protection of minorities, it is desirable that the President and two Members appointed by him in each case should proceed to consider any petition or communication addressed to the League of Nations with regard to an infraction, or danger of infraction, of the clauses of the Treaties for the protection of minorities. This inquiry would be held as soon as the petition or communication in question had been brought to the notice of the Members of the Council.'

3. *Resolution adopted by the Council on June 27th, 1921*

With reference to M. Tittoni's report, adopted on October 22nd, 1920, at Brussels, the Council of the League of Nations resolves that:

'All petitions concerning the protection of minorities under the provisions of the Treaties from petitioners other than Members of the League of Nations shall be immediately communicated to the State concerned.

'The State concerned shall be bound to inform the Secretary-General, within three weeks of the date upon which its representative accredited to the Secretariat of the League of Nations received the text of the petition in question, whether it intends to make any comments on the subject.

'Should the State concerned not reply within the period of three weeks, or should it state that it does not propose to make any comments, the petition in question shall be communicated to the Members of the League of Nations in accordance with the procedure laid down in M. Tittoni's report.

'Should the State concerned announce that it wishes to submit comments, a period of two months, dating from the day on which its representative accredited to the Secretariat of the League receives the text of the petition, shall be granted to it for this purpose. The Secretary-General, on receipt of the comments, shall communicate the petition, together with the comments, to the Members of the League of Nations.

'In exceptional and extremely urgent cases, the Secretary-General shall, before communicating the petition to the Members of the League of Nations, inform the representative accredited to the Secretariat of the League of Nations by the State concerned.

'This decision shall come into immediate effect for all matters affecting Poland and Czechoslovakia.

'With regard to other States which have accepted the Treaty provisions relating to the protection of minorities, the Council authorizes the Secretary-General to inform them of the decision taken in the case of Czechoslovakia and Poland and to ask them to state whether they wish the same procedure to be made applicable to them.'

4. *Resolution adopted by the Council on September 5th, 1923*

With reference to the previous resolutions relating to the procedure to be followed with regard to the protection of minorities, dated October 22nd and 25th, 1920, and June 27th, 1921, the Council of the League of Nations decides that:

1. In order that they may be submitted to the procedure established by the Council resolutions, dated October 22nd and 25th, 1920, and June 27th, 1921, petitions addressed to the League of Nations concerning the protection of minorities:

(*a*) Must have in view the protection of minorities in accordance with the Treaties;

(*b*) In particular, must not be submitted in the form of a request for the severance of political relations between the minority in question and State of which it forms a part;

(*c*) Must not emanate from an anonymous or unauthenticated source;

(*d*) Must abstain from violent language;

(*e*) Must contain information or refer to facts which have not recently been the subject of a petition submitted to the ordinary procedure.

If the interested State raises for any reason an objection against the acceptance of a petition, the Secretary-General shall submit the question of acceptance to the President of the Council, who may invite two other Members of the Council to assist him in the consideration of this question. If the State concerned so requests, this question of procedure shall be included in the agenda of the Council.

2. The extension of the period of two months, fixed by the resolution of June 27th, 1921, for observations by the Government concerned on the subject of the petitions may be authorized by the President of the Council if the State concerned so requests and if the circumstances appear to make such a course necessary and feasible.

3. The communication, in accordance with the resolution of June 27th, 1921, to the Members of the League of petitions and of observations (should there be any) by the Government concerned shall be restricted to the Members of the Council. Communications may be made to other Members of the League or to the general public at the request of the State concerned, or by virtue of a resolution to this effect passed by the Council after the matter has been duly submitted to it.

4. The consideration of petitions and observations (should there be any) of the Governments concerned by the President and two other Members of the Council, in accordance with the resolution of October 25th, 1920, shall be undertaken with the sole object of determining whether one or more Members of the Council should draw the attention of the Council to an infraction, or danger of an infraction, of the clauses of the Treaties for the protection of minorities. The right reserved to all Members of the Council of drawing its attention to an infraction, or danger of infraction, remains unaffected.

5. The present resolution shall be communicated to the Governments which have signed treaties or made declarations concerning the protection of minorities.

5. Resolution adopted by the Council on June 10th, 1925

The Council of the League of Nations,

Considering that, by the resolution of October 25th, 1920, it was decided, with a view to assisting Members of the Council in the exercise of their rights and duties as regards the protection of minorities, that it is desirable that the President and two members appointed by him in each case should proceed to consider any petition or communication addressed to the League of Nations with regard to an infraction or danger of infraction of the clauses of the Treaties for the protection of minorities, and that this inquiry should be held as soon as the petition or communication in question has been brought to the notice of the Members of the Council,

Decides

I. If the Acting President of the Council is:

The representative of the State of which the persons belonging to the minority in question are subjects, or

The representative of a neighbouring State of the State to which the persons belonging to the minority in question are subject; or

The representative of a State the majority of whose population belong from the ethnical point of view to the same people as the persons belonging to the minority in question,
that the duty which falls upon the President of the Council in accordance with the terms of the resolution of October 25th, 1920, shall be performed by the Member of the Council who exercised the duties of President immediately before the Acting President, and who is not in the same position.

II. The President of the Council, in appointing two of his colleagues in conformity with the resolution of October 25th, 1920, shall not appoint either the representative of the State to which the persons belonging to the minority in question are subject, or the representative of a State neighbouring the State to which these persons are subject, or the representative of a State a majority of whose population belong from the ethnical point of view to the same people as the persons in question.

6. *Resolution adopted by the Council on June 13th, 1929*

The Council:

(*a*) Decides to add to the provisions contained in its previous resolutions regarding the procedure for the examination of minorities petitions the following provisions:

1. Receivability of Petitions.

When the Secretary-General declares a petition non-receivable, he will inform the petitioner and, if necessary, will communicate to him the Council resolution of September 5th, 1923, laying down the conditions of receivability of minorities petitions.

2. Composition of Minorities Committees.

The President of the Council may, in exceptional cases, invite four Members of the Council to examine minorities petitions instead of two as laid down in the Council resolution of October 25th, 1920.

3. Frequency of the Meetings of the Minorities Committees.

The Council considers that it would be desirable for Minorities Committees to take into account the possibility of holding meetings in the intervals between sessions of the Council, whenever they think it expedient for the examination of individual petitions.

4. Communications concerning the Action taken on Petitions by the Minorities Committees.

(i) When the members of a Minorities Committee have finished the examination of a question, without asking that it be placed on the Council's agenda, they will communicate the result of their examination by letter to the other Members of the Council for their information. The Secretary-General will keep the relevant documents at the disposal of the Members of the Council.

(ii) The Secretary-General will distribute once a year, for the information of all the Members of the Council, a document reproducing the letters addressed during the year, as described above, by the various Minorities Committees to the Members of the Council.

Index of Persons Mentioned in the Main Body of the Text

József Galántai

József Galántai is professor of history at Budapest's Eötvös Loránd University, where he has taught since his graduation in 1952. His research areas are Hungarian and East Central European history in the nineteenth and twentieth centuries, the Dual Monarchy, and problems of historiography. He was appointed a professor in 1972, and in the following year was awarded the prestigious Academy of Sciences Prize.

Professor Galántai has written numerous books on modern history including *Magyarország az első világháborúban* (Hungary in the First World War), 1964; *Az 1867-es kiegyezés* (The Compromise of 1867), 1967; *A Habsburg monarchia alkonya* (The Decline of the Habsburg Monarchy), 1985; and *A trianoni békekötés 1920* (The Trianon Peace Settlement, 1920), 1990. The present work appeared in Hungarian in 1989.

Volumes Published by Atlantic Research and Publications
"Studies on Society in Change"

No. 1   *Tolerance and Movements of Religious Dissent in Eastern Europe.* Edited by Béla K. Király 1977.

No. 2   *The Habsburg Empire in World War I.* Edited by R.A. Kann. 1978.

No. 3   *The Mutual Effects of the Islamic and Judeo-Christian Worlds: The East European Pattern.* Edited by A. Ascher, T. Halasi-Kun, B. K. Király 1979.

No. 4   *Before Watergate: Problems of Corruption in American Society.* Edited by A.S. Eisenstadt. A. Hoogenboom, H.L. Trefousse. 1979.

No. 5   *East Central European Perceptions of Early America.* Edited by B. K. Király and G. Barány 1977.

No. 6   *The Hungarian Revolution of 1956 in Retrospect.* Edited by B. K. Király and Paul Jonas. 1978.

No. 7   *Brooklyn, U.S.A.: Fourth Largest City in America.* Edited by Rita S. Miller. 1979.

No. 8   *Prime Minister Gyula Andrássy's Influence on Habsburg Foreign Policy.* János Décsy. 1979.

No. 9   *The Great Impeacher: A Political Biography of James M. Ashley.* Robert F. Horowitz. 1979.

Vol. I[1]
No. 10   *Special Topics and Generalizations on the Eighteenth and Nineteenth Century.* Edited by Béla K. Király and Gunther E. Rothenberg. 1979.

Vol. II
No. 11   *East Central European Society and War in the Pre-Revolutionary 18th Century Europe.* Edited by Gunther E. Rothenberg, Béla K. Király, and Peter F. Sugar. 1982.

Vol. III
No. 12   *From Hunyadi to Rákoczy: War and Society in Late Medieval and Early Modern Hungary.* Edited by János Bak and Béla K. Király. 1982.

---

[1] Volumes I through XXVIII refer to the series *War and Society in East Central Europe.*

Vol. IV

No. 13   *East Central European Society and War in the Era of Revolutions: 1775–1856.* Edited by B. K. Király. 1984.

Vol. V

No. 14   *Essays On World War 1: Origins and Prisoners of War.* Edited by Samuel R. Williamson, Jr. and Peter Pastor. 1983.

Vol. VI

No. 15   *Essays on World War I: Total War and Peacemaking. A Case Study on Trianon.* Edited by B. K. Király, Peter Pastor, and Ivan Sanders. 1982.

Vol. VII

No. 16   *Army, Aristocracy, Monarchy: War, Society, and Government in Austria, 1618–1780.* Thomas M. Barker. 1982.

Vol. VIII

No. 17   *The First Serbian Uprising 1804–1813.* Edited by Wayne S. Vucinich. 1982.

Vol. IX

No. 18   *Czechoslovak Policy and the Hungarian Minority 1945–1948.* By Kálmán Janics, Edited by Stephen Borsody. 1982.

Vol. X

No. 19   *At The Brink of War and Peace: The Tito-Stalin Split in Historic Perspective.* Edited by Wayne S. Vucinich. 1982.

No. 20   *Inflation Through the Ages: Economic, Social, Psychological, and Historical Aspects.* Edited by Edward Marcus and Nathan Schmuckler. 1981.

No. 21   *Germany and America: Essays on Problems of International Relations and Immigration.* Edited by Hans L. Trefousse. 1980.

No. 22   *Brooklyn College: The First Half Century.* Murray M. Horowitz. 1981.

No. 23   *A New Deal for the World: Eleanor Roosevelt and American Foreign Policy.* Jason Berger. 1981.

No. 24   *The Legacy of Jewish Migration: 1881 and Its Impact.* Edited by David Berger. 1982.

No. 25   *The Road to Bellapais: Cypriot Exodus to Northern Cyprus.* Pierre Oberling. 1982.

No. 26   *New Hungarian Peasants: An East Central European Experience with Collectivization.* Edited by Marida Hollos and Béla C. Maday. 1983.

No. 27   *Germans in America: Aspects of German-American Relations in the Nineteenth Century.* Edited by Allen McCormick. 1983.

No. 28   *A Question of Empire: Leopold I and the War of Spanish Succession, 1701–1705.* Linda and Marsha Frey. 1983.

No. 29   *The Beginning of Cyrillic Printing- Cracow, 1491. From the Orthodox Past in Poland.* Edited by Ludwik Krzyzanowski. 1983.

No. 29a   *A Grand Ecole for the Grand Corps: The Recruitment and Training of the French Administration.* Thomas R. Osborne. 1983.

Vol. XI
No. 30   *The First War Between Socialist States: The Hungarian Revolution of 1956 and Its Impact.* Edited by Béla K. Király, Barbara Lotze, and Nandor Dreisziger. 1984.

Vol. XII
No. 31   *The Effects of World War I: The Uprooted Hungarian Refugees and Their Impact on Hungary's Domestic Policies.* István Mócsy. 1983.

Vol. XIII
No. 32   *The Effects of World War I: The Class War After the Great War: The Rise of Communist Parties in East Central Europe, 1918–1921.* Edited by Ivo Banac. 1983.

Vol. XIV
No. 33   *The Crucial Decade: East Central European Society and National Defense 1859–1870.* Edited by B. K. Király. 1984.

Vol. XVI
No. 35   *The Effects of World War I: War and Communism in Hungary, 1919.* György Péteri. 1984.

Vol. XVII
No. 36   *Insurrections, Wars, and the Eastern Crisis in the 1870s.* Edited by B. K. Király and Gale Stokes. 1985.

Vol. XVIII
No. 37   *East Central European Society and the Balkan Wars, 1912–1913.* Edited by B. K. Király and Dmitrije Djordjevic. 1986.

Vol. XIX
No. 38   *East Central European Society in World War I.* Edited by B. K. Király and N.F. Dreisziger, Assistant Editor Albert A. Nofi. 1985.

Vol. XX
No. 39   *Revolutions and Interventions in Hungary and Its Neighboring States, 1918–1919.* Edited by Peter Pastor. 1988.

Vol. XXI
No. 40   *East Central European Society and War, 1750–1920. Bibliography and Historiography.* Compiled and Edited by László Alföldi. Pending.

Vol. XXII
No. 41   *Essays on East Central European Society and War: 1740s–1920s.* Edited by Stephen Fischer-Galati and Béla K. Király. 1988.

Vol. XXIII
No. 42   *East Central European Maritime Commerce and Naval Policies,*

1789–1913. Edited by Apostolos E. Vacalopoulos, Constantinos D. Svolopoulos, and Béla K. Király. 1989.

Vol. XXIV

No. 43 *Selection, Social Origins, Education and Training of East Central European Officers Corps.* Edited by Béla K. Király and Walter Scott Dillard. 1988.

Vol. XXV

No. 44 *East Central European War Leaders: Civilian and Military.* Edited by Béla K. Király and Albert Nofi. 1988.

No. 46 *Germany's International Monetary Policy and the European Monetary System.* Hugo Kaufmann. 1985.

No. 47 *Iran Since the Revolution- Internal Dynamics, Regional Conflicts and the Superpowers.* Edited by Barry M. Rosen. 1985.

Vol. XXVII

No. 48 *The Press During the Hungarian Revolution of 1848–1849.* Domokos Kosáry. 1986.

No. 49 *The Spanish Inquisition and the Inquisitional Mind.* Edited by Angel Alcala. 1987.

No. 50 *Catholics, the State and the European Radical Right, 1919–1945.* Edited by Richard Wolff and Jorg K. Hoensch. 1987.

Vol. XXVIII

No. 51 *The Boer War and Military Reform.* Jay Stone and Erwin A. Schmidl. 1987.

No. 52 *Baron Joseph Eötvös, A Literary Biography.* Steven B. Várdy. 1987.

No. 53 *Towards the Renaissance of Puerto Rican Studies: Ethnic and Area Studies in University Education.* Maria Sanchez and Antonio M. Stevens. 1987.

No. 54 *The Brazilian Diamonds in Contracts, Contraband and Capital.* Harry Bernstein. 1987.

No. 55 *Christians, Jews and Other Worlds: Patterns of Conflict and Accommodation.* Edited by Philip F. Gallagher. 1988.

Vol. XXVI

No. 56 *The Fall of the Medieval Kingdom of Hungary: Mohács, 1526, Buda, 1541.* Géza Perjés. 1989.

No. 57 *The Lord Mayor of Lisbon: The Portugese Tribune of the People and His Twenty-four Guilds.* Harry Bernstein. 1989.

No. 58   *Hungarian Statesmen of Destiny: 1860–1960.* Edited by Paul Bódy. 1989.

No. 59   *For China: The Memoirs of T. G. Li, Former Major General in the Chinese Nationalist Army.* T. G. Li. Written in collaboration with Roman Rome. 1989.

No. 60   *Politics in Hungary: For a Democratic Alternative.* János Kis, with an Introduction by Timothy Garton Ash. 1989.

No. 61   *Hungarian Worker's Councils in 1956.* Edited by Bill Lomax. 1990.

No. 62   *Essays on the Structure and Reform of Centrally Planned Economic Systems.* Paul Jonas. 1990.

No. 63.   Éva H. Haraszti, *Kossuth as a Journalist in England*
A joint publication with Akadémiai Kiadó, Budapest. 1991.

No. 64.   Máriai Ormos, *From Padua to the Trianon, 1918–1920*
A joint publication with Akadémiai Kiadó, Budapest. 1991.

No. 65.   László Gerevich, ed., *Towns in Medieval Hungary*
A joint publication with Akadémiai Kiadó, Budapest. 1991.

No. 66.   Sándor Bíró, *The Nationalities Problem in Transylvania, 1867–1940. 1991.*

No. 67.   Béla Borsi-Kálmán, *Hungarian Exiles and the Romanian National Movement, 1849–1867. 1991.*

No. 68.   Rudolf Joó and Andrew Ludanyi, eds., *The Hungarian Minority's Situation in Ceausescu's Romania. 1991.*

No. 69.   István Bibó, *Democracy, Revolution, Self Determination. Selected Writings. 1991.*

No. 70.   József Galántai, *Trianon and the Protection of Minorities*
A joint publication with Corvina Kiadó, Budapest. 1992.

No. 71.   György Györffy, *King Saint Stephen of Hungary*
A joint publication with Corvina Kiadó, Budapest. In preparation.

No. 72.   Robert A. Kann, *Dynasty, Politics, and Culture. Selected Essays.* In preparation.

No. 73.   Oscar Halceki, *Jadwiga of Anjou and the Rise of East Central Europe*
A joint publication with the Polish Institute of Arts and Sciences of America. In preparation.